Superta

William Gilbert worked at sea for over thirty years, travelling all over the world on tankers, freighters and eventually superyachts, while simultaneously pursuing a career as a professional writer.

OTHER WORKS BY WILLIAM GILBERT

Novels

Supertanker Port of Call Asia

Supertanker Port of Call Cartagena

Supertanker Port of Call San Francisco

Pink Taxi

The Captain's Daughter

Short Stories

Supertanker Captain and other stories

London Transport, Tales of London Life

Travel and other writings

Cuba Port of Call

SUPERTANKER CIRCUMNAVIGATION

BY

WILLIAM GILBERT

www.captainwilliamgilbert.com

Book cover design by The Book Design House
www.thebookdesignhouse.com

Contents

Houston	7
To Panama and the canal	22
The Pacific	31
Japan	52
Tank cleaning	66
Singapore	78
Return to Yokohama	102
To Jeddah	104
The Suez Canal and the Mediterranean	125
The Atlantic and the storm	129
New Jersey	133
To the Gulf and Houston	139

Supertanker Circumnavigation

Houston

The ship was long and still in ballast, the rust-red-coloured boot-topping showing. The paint on her upper hull was so rust-streaked that it blended in with the boot-topping in places.

The gang of sailors, in the middle of which I stood, seemed to look upon her with despair. "So much for the new tonnage," said one, quietly.

A few of the American workers wandered up and down the quay, looking scruffy in their flannel shirts and trainers. They ignored us. "Hi," I said to one in an attempt to start a conversation. He didn't even look round.

"Tossers," said one of the sailors.

Finally, the cook sighed and went over to the accommodation ladder and started climbing it, holding his bag up over his head. He didn't seem to have brought much for a five-month voyage. The rest of us followed him.

At the top, we passed some Scandinavian seamen, smiling broadly, who were hustling their luggage out onto the deck, and then we entered the ship's accommodation.

We found ourselves in the saloon, a bare

room with a dining table which reminded me of my old air cadet squadron's hut. A solid-looking man in his thirties sat there. He didn't look up. "Leave your seamen's books on the table," he said. The sailors did so and left. They seemed to know where they were going and what to do. I and the other cadet just stood there.

Eventually, the man looked up with an enquiring expression. "Are you two cadets or something?" he said, contemptuously.

"Yeah," said the other cadet. This was the only time he would address this man in such a manner. He was quickly put in his place. This was the captain, a solid, 'I were brought up in paper bag in t'street', type from Yorkshire. He didn't like being spoken to like that by a teenager joining for his first trip.

"Go and find the mate," he said, eventually. We left and stood outside the saloon door, wondering in which direction we should turn. "He'll be in the cargo room," said the captain.

We bimbled around and found a slightly younger man sitting in a room full of out-of-date-looking control panels. "So, you're here," he said. Another Northerner. I was a Southerner. I was beginning to feel a bit out of place. The Merchant Navy doesn't take many Southerners. They don't need to work on scruffy tankers. Southerners are positioned to get nice jobs in the City of London and if they really want to go to sea, the Royal Navy will take them and their nice accents as officers, or the cruise companies will, which, while technically part of the Merchant Navy, can't really be considered to be part of the same world as that of the cargo ship companies.

The mate seemed more cheerful than the captain. Twenty years later, when I finally became a captain, I was able to understand why this would be. A captain lives with huge responsibility and the daily threat of criminal prosecution for innumerable offences almost none of which would be his fault and it's a very solitary life. The mate can still have a modicum of fun. Generally, if there's a disaster, he is just fired; jail doesn't appear on the horizon.

He took us to our cabins. I was surprised to find that we had our own cabins. This wasn't, as it turned out, an act of generosity. Since companies had started to go over to minimum manning and abandon non-essential maintenance, all the older ships had spare cabins galore. At one stage, later in the trip, when the sailors were chipping paint with air tools, I was to alternate between two cabins, one on each side of the ship, depending upon on which side they were working, and no one even noticed.

The mate issued us with bright orange boiler suits and safety boots and sat us down and asked what they'd told us at our induction course at college.

"Eh, not much," I said. "They kept banging on about tank rescues." The mate smiled.

"Oh yeah," he said. "Don't worry about that. You can forget it. If you're going down a tank, you're going to get a corpse." It turned out that this is, actually, true and his attitude would have saved lives in a tank disaster situation, not cost them, but more on that later. He seemed to think that this answer should be regarded in a positive light.

The second mate came in. He looked younger than the mate and older at the same time, as if he had that genetic deformity some children are born with, owing to which they age prematurely. We were to find out that he was a borderline alcoholic. It was a shame, because this guy turned out to be highly professional and a very good officer, apart from that.

At the time, they hadn't yet had the big cover-up of the true causes of the Exxon Valdez disaster in which they blamed it all on the captain's drinking and so there wasn't much of a problem with alcoholism in the eyes of the companies and the authorities. In fact, there was a belief among some that the companies actually looked in favour upon alcoholics as the alcoholics couldn't survive working ashore because they couldn't afford the amount of alcohol they wanted on the salary which they would receive in the menial jobs which were all Merchant Navy deck officers with such specialised qualifications could get, especially as it would have to be duty paid. They were, then, kind of like indentured labour.

We were sent out on deck. The ship would soon be moving along the Houston ship canal. There wasn't enough depth of water to load alongside at this berth.

The deck was two hundred yards long, and little pools of hydraulic oil surrounded the stems of the tank valves, and you had to be careful walking along not to slide and fall flat on your face onto the steel plate. Sawdust had been strewn liberally in the places where the valves had been leaking for a while, but in other places there was none.

The second mate was busily organising

things. We tried to help but didn't know what he wanted us to do and he was too tired to instruct us. He just sighed every time we did something he hadn't wanted us to do.

Around midday, he went inside and the third mate came out. He was a jollier character. He liked his job. We found out later that the mate considered him to be incompetent and loathed him, and he in turn loathed the mate, believing him to be excessively officious, but, at the time, we were blissfully ignorant of all these undercurrents and their associated political machinations.

The Scandinavians from whom we were taking over the ship left the vessel and the pilots came onboard. I was quite surprised. They were scruffy, just like the stevedores. They were very loud and bumptious.

The third mate went away to the bridge with them and then returned. "Right, we're moving," he said. "Who wants to go up forward with the mate and who wants to go aft with the second mate?"

"I'll go aft," I said. The other cadet trooped up forward and I went to the poop. The third mate went up to the bridge.

The second mate and some of the sailors were on the poop. They were moving huge ropes around. It took two or three men to lug them. There were wires too but these were on winches.

Mooring operations on these big ships were quite dangerous. Sailors got their legs caught in bights and ripped off; wires broke and whipped back and decapitated people. It was slowly dawning on me just how dangerous working in the Merchant Navy was. The sailors were never to complain about safety though, in my experience. They complained about everything else but never that. I couldn't work out why. They were on such low pay and the management were so vicious and ruthless that you'd think they would harp on with their most legitimate cause for complaint, but they never did. I suppose they were part of the same tradition as the men who went uncomplainingly aloft in a gale to furl the mainsail.

Suddenly, the second mate got a radio message and I was sent up to the bridge. "I thought you should take turns being up here during manoeuvres," said the captain, when I arrived. I quickly found out that I had really been sent up to make the tea.

I was just boiling the kettle when I heard the senior pilot say to the sailor on the wheel, "You do exactly as he says." I turned to see that the senior pilot was pointing at the junior pilot. The sailor looked offended. He was a Geordie who'd been at sea on tankers for ten years and didn't need to be told his duties by some American. He looked over at the captain, and a flicker of communication passed between them. I don't know if he was asking the captain for permission to punch the pilot's lights out or something. Then he turned to the pilot, "Do you think...," he began. The captain interrupted him. "He understands," said the captain. The senior pilot looked confused. I think he was used to talking to third-world seamen who, mindful of the thirty or so relatives whom each was supporting back at home, took any abuse directed at them without complaint.

Having made the tea and coffee, I was stationed at one of the bridge doors to relay orders from the junior pilot to the wheelman.

The senior pilot stood next to me. Unfortunately, I was unfamiliar with the standard orders and the junior pilot had such a strong Southern American accent that I couldn't understand him. There were two very similar-sounding orders, 'stop her' and 'starboard'. Obviously, starboard usually had an angle attached. Still, despite that, I was confused. The pilot pronounced stop her and starboard exactly the same, to my ears. The senior pilot would interpret and I would then relay the order to the wheelman. It would have been a lot easier if the senior pilot had just passed the orders directly to the wheelman but I suppose that wouldn't have been considered right.

The ship moved along the canal, assisted by two tugs. The captain got on great with the pilots. He was a bluff, hugely-confident man himself, so these full-of-themselves Americans and he suited each other. He later said that the Houston ship canal guys were excellent pilots and that he truly admired them. I suppose they had to be good, moving ships up and down there, turning them short round, mooring them between buoys.

The tugs turned us and brought us into our spot and we tied up. The pilots left the bridge, and I spotted one of their official caps lying on the console. I gave it to the captain. He went over to the bridge wing, saw them disappearing on their pilot boat, smiled, and put it on his head.

The mate was full throttle now. Loading was a very critical time. The second mate had been sent to bed and we were working with the third mate again. The hours these guys were doing were quite evil. They were on six hours on, six hours off, but if there were anything exceptional happening, such as manoeuvering, they were dragged out of bed. This schedule could go on for days or weeks in port. Since then, the International Maritime Organisation, a body whose endless legislation in the name of safety normally has unintended consequences which actually make life at sea even more dangerous, in my opinion, has brought in some rules to prevent over-tiredness among seamen, not, I believe, out of any concern for the seamen, but out of concern for the environment which tends to suffer if seamen make mistakes. There is really only lip service paid to all this. If seamen complain about their hours, they will suffer. All the rules basically mean is that the authorities and the company have protected themselves and if there is any incident and they find out that the seaman had been overtired because his working hours exceeded the maximum stated in the regulations, they simply point the finger at the captain for allowing the rules to be broken on his ship. The fact that if they weren't, the ship would never get from A to B, the company would go bankrupt and the wives of all the IMO officials would never have any fuel to take their kids to private school in their 4x4's is considered to be irrelevant.

The Houston ship canal was fascinating. It was full of traffic. Barges brought their loads out to us and pumped it into our tanks. The barge men drawled when they spoke and seemed to take half an hour to say a sentence. Some of them clambered onboard and sprawled in chairs in the cargo room, providing a contrast with the upright figure of the mate.

I was looking over the rail at one stage

and I saw the barge operator taking puffs on a cigarette while he was checking the tanks. Our entire ship was plastered with no-smoking signs, and so, when the mate appeared, I pointed this out to him. He wasn't bothered. We didn't have any jurisdiction over the barges, though if they blew up, they'd take us out, too. "Tossers," said the sailor who'd said this earlier on the quay. "They always have been." I thought this was a bit harsh. The Texans on board seemed friendly enough.

At lunchtime, I and the third mate handed over to the second mate and the other cadet. Somehow, we cadets had slipped into this six on six off mode. This was a blunder. On this schedule, we were always too tired to learn anything. If we'd sort of floated the idea earlier past the mate that we might be on daywork, perhaps just a little subliminal suggestion, we might not have been put on this six on six off schedule.

Sailors had used to work equal time on, equal time off until Captain Cook sorted it out. He reasoned that fatigue was killing them and that it'd be better to have a crew who were on a lighter schedule, but were still alive. Modern shipping company managers didn't share his benign attitude.

There'd been a policy until fairly recently of letting the cadets have as much time off as possible in port with a view to encouraging longevity of employment but since the crews had been cut down, the mates were leaving them on duty as much as possible. The mates didn't care if they wore them out or they got so dispirited that they left. The company could just hire some new kids.

We were on two hundred and seventy-five pounds a month, some of which came from government subsidies, so we were cheap labour.

Gradually, the tanks were filled. The second mate and the third mate were not getting on. The second mate would always leave all the tanks filled to a certain pattern so that they were staggered and when a tank needed topping off, it was a simple matter. The third mate left them filled to more or less random levels, and the second mate would have to spend all his watch getting the whole thing sorted out again.

The third mate had done his training on cargo ships and passenger ships; the second mate had done his on tankers, so he was better at this sort of thing.

The sailors themselves weren't of much assistance with cargo loading. They were just there, really, to do the heavy lifting, the mooring, and to be lookouts. At sea, the sailors on duty who were not working as lookouts would chip rust, an endless job which was quite pointless as the ship was so big and there were so few of them that they couldn't really make a difference and as soon as they'd chipped paint, the metal got a layer of salt on it, so the new paint went straight onto that and within a few weeks of repainting the area being worked was in a worse state than it had been before. But they had to be kept occupied.

They were mainly ex B.P. and Shell men. They seemed to think fairly well of B.P. The sailors from that company were just a little resentful that they'd be replaced with Filipinos and referred to B.P. as The British Philippino company. The company they all seemed to really hate, including the ones who'd never worked for it, was Shell. I just got the impression that they thought the company was overly officious. There was a term for people who'd worked on their ships: shell-shocked. To be fair though, Shell didn't seem to have made their guys redundant; their sailors just left to escape working for Shell anymore, willingly taking a pay cut.

The third mate was ex-P and O. He hated them. "I was a model cadet," he said. "I loved having the house badge on my blazer and all that, then I was made redundant as soon as I got my ticket even though I went to the Falklands with them during the war. I was on the S.S. Uganda. The Canberra boys all got jobs, but I didn't, and the training manager had the cheek to say to me I'd had it easy because I hadn't been in the thick of it like the Canberra boys, but the Uganda made two runs into San Carlos sound." We nodded understandingly while he railed against the unfairness of all this.

They switched my hours around and accompanied the sailors on a run ashore. I was quite tired but I thought, what did I join the Merchant Navy for if I'm not going to see anything. This little sortie would mean staying awake for about twenty hours, fifteen or so of them on duty.

We went to Gillie's, a big Western style nightclub that I think was the one used in the film Urban Cowboy.

I thought it was a bit odd. The guys wore straw hats and skipped around with the girls, doing this sort of barn dance. I thought it looked a bit gay, actually, but I suppose it must have been a lot more fun than the moronic shuffling of one's weight from one foot to the other that passes for dancing in an English nightclub.

No one wanted to speak to us. I don't think they liked sailors.

While we waited outside the club for a taxi back, the sailors spied a gun shop. We all walked over to it. The hardware in the window was quite formidable. I found it strange: all the fuss over our I.D.s before we could buy alcohol and yet you could buy a machine gun without any problem. Still, I suppose if you were going to let the public have machine guns, best to monitor their drinking quite studiously.

Suddenly, another of the sailors spied a strip club and our return to the ship was postponed for a little while. I've always thought that strip clubs were a complete waste of money. What is the point in paying a fortune to be teased by women in bikinis and get beaten up by the bouncers if you touch them when you can go to the beach and be teased by women in bikinis for free and get beaten up by the police if you touch them. My opinion wouldn't have counted for very much though, so I quietly trailed along after them.

Once inside, one of the more vicious sailors told me to go and put a dollar in a stripper's G-string. I was reluctant but he insisted.

The girl was quite gorgeous and once I put the dollar in her G-string, she stopped twirling and leant down and started a conversation with me. Blushing over the attention, I explained that we were from an oil tanker. She said something like, "That's wonderful, honey," and I went back to the sailors. The vicious one was not happy. He'd wanted me embarrassed and humiliated and instead I'd kind of been chatted-up by the stripper.

Once on the ship again, we continued working. We were getting bitten by these evil mosquitoes. Their bites aren't like the bites of European mosquitoes. If they bite you on your hand, it swells up to twice its size. There is one very good spray, incidentally, American, but we didn't have any. God forbid that the company would think to put mosquito repellent on board.

I was bitten on one hand and it swelled up so much that it became difficult to swing the valves, but I just about coped.

I was standing the next morning with the second mate during the handover and the bosun walked past. He was a big guy with a, Nigel Mansell, policeman's-style, black moustache. "I don't like you," he said to me, stopping briefly. "You're a weirdo."

"I prefer the term eccentric," I said.

"I prefer the term weirdo," he insisted. Then he went on his way. The second mate laughed.

"Don't worry about him." He said. "You'll be glad of him if these A.B.s start playing-up."

"Beat them up, will he?" I asked.

"Knock them flat on their faces," said the second mate. "I've seen him do it. It's quite impressive. You need someone like that. Some of these A.B.s have got records for stuff like grievous bodily harm, as long as your arm."

The second mate and the bosun got on. I could never work out why. The second mate liked a drink and was frequently drunk and was an affable character; the bosun was taciturn, never started any sort of conversation and I never saw him drunk.

Eventually, we were full. Some more-senior refinery people came on board; the mate did his calculations. At this time, everything was more or less manual. There was no computer. The tank levels were measured with little weights on tapes, encased in housings so that you didn't have to open a lid and get a face full of fumes to get the measurements. Then, with these figures, the mate would enter endless tables and work out the volume of cargo on board. It wasn't simple. You had to take into account the temperature, the fact that the weights would float at different levels, depending on the density of the cargo etc... etc... The mate was highly intelligent, though, and flew through the calculations.

We were doing all right. The refinery's surveyors and the mate didn't have any disagreements. We hadn't been faced with a U.S. Coastguard inspection.

The U.S. Coastguard are a total pain. Their people go on and on about how brilliant they, themselves, are but the American penchant for excessive regulation and the lack of practical experience of a lot of their guys makes dealing with them very difficult.

Finally, we were cleared to leave. Tugs were made fast, the pilots were on board, and we slipped our lines from the mooring buoys.

We were leaving at night, and I was up forward this time. The sight was just fantastic. I believe they've cleaned the place up a bit now but, at the time, the refineries were free to burn off all the waste gasses, and sailing down the canal was like sailing through a sea of fire. The scene reminded me of Bladerunner. I truly thought it was the eighth wonder of the world.

Once the pilots were off and the tugs gone, we were sent to bed. At last, after a week on this sixes torture, we were on daywork.

To Panama and the canal

I woke up in the morning and went out on deck. We didn't seem to be moving. When I went back inside, I bumped into the mate. "We're at anchor, broken down," he said.

"So much for the new tonnage," I could hear the cook saying to the steward in the galley.

We were sent outside to assist the crew. They were moving things around and tying things up. The Scandinavians had left the ship a complete disaster. They were, said the captain, good at operating ships, but not good at maintaining them. I was a little confused by this statement. Weren't they two aspects of the same thing.

The surly bosun had me help him tie some seizings on a few things. I did some and asked him if they were right. I was trying to remember how we did it on our month's induction course at Warsash School of Navigation. "There is no official method of seizing," he said. "I just assumed that you'd do it right. Stupid of me really." I said nothing in my defence, but there is an official method. They had shown it to us, and it was in a little booklet.

I was standing with the jolly third mate while he was nattering away when the mate came up to me and said, "If you're not happy, you can get off in Panama." I was mystified. I was quite happy. I hadn't said anything. What was he on about. It turned out that he'd gone into my cabin and there were a few things strewn about and he'd decided that this showed a general bad attitude. I was beginning to think that the captain was the only totally sane, normal, person on the boat.

At least the third mate was, I thought, a happy soul. Then, out of the blue, he started ranting about Jews. I was mystified. He was from the West Country. Did any Jews even live in the West Country. I mentioned this to the second mate later on. "Oh yeah," said the second mate. "He's half-German. Occasionally, he just goes off on one. Just ignore him, and he'll soon return to normal."

We sailed down to Panama, once the engineers had got the engine going again. The British engineers were quite surprised to find, once they'd started attacking the engine with their tools, that it was green. It'd been covered in so much grime that they'd thought it was black. I didn't understand how the Scandinavians reconciled this state of affairs with all the literature they left lying around claiming their company was just wonderful.

It was quite peaceful and balmy out in the Gulf and we were out of range of the mosquitoes. My hand was beginning to return to normal size and I could manipulate it fairly easily again.

We soon found out what was going to be our biggest bugbear on the trip, study. There was this vague, general idea that cadets should be studying. We had a bit of a correspondence course from Warsash which wasn't very challenging, but there were other things to study, too. There was no definitive list, though. The mates were all too tired or busy to teach us or had not done some things such as sextant navigation for so long that they had forgotten how to, and they'd had no teacher training, obviously and, so, were really bad at explaining things. The mate would take the time to explain some things, but he was so rigid he might bombard you with twenty questions once he'd finished his explanation and if you only got nineteen right, he would just explode with rage and start fuming, shouting things such as, "I'm wasting my time with you!"

The tiring thing was that if you ever did anything off duty such as flick through a magazine, it was always, "You've no time for that, you should be studying." They had a stick to beat you with.

There was a small volume called, colloquially, the collision regulations, which was a bit of a misnomer as it was really the anti-collision regulations. If you could quote this at your oral exam in three years' time, your chances of passing increased dramatically, so I decided to just get on with memorising it.

After a few days, we anchored off Colon in Panama. The captain wasn't laying on any boats, so we couldn't go ashore. I met someone later who'd been ashore there with a Filipino crew. They'd taken him to a club with a stage show in which the opening performance was a timid Indian girl being more or less raped by a big black guy and the finale was a donkey show, so it didn't sound too salubrious. There were no dilemmas over whether I should accompany the crew thanks to the captain's parsimony with the expenses and refusal to lay on the boats, and so

I didn't have to consider all the warnings which the officers had delivered on this subject.

I went out on the starboard side and looked out at the shore lights, while, unseen in the shadows, I listened to the bosun and the steward talking about old times.

They were all romantics, these sailors: violent, unpredictable, occasionally irrational men, but all romantics. They were the kind of men driven out of society now. In the age of the Tony Blair types, there was no place for them, anymore. And these were the last of their kind: the British deep-sea merchant seaman other ranks. It was a shame; an entire tradition was on its way out.

The next morning, the pilots came on board and we went through the canal. The pilots were American. They were obnoxious American tough guys, another type who are on their way out. Nowadays, guys like them get in one bar fight, get thrown in jail, get approached by the Aryan Nation, kill someone for the Aryan Nation, and then are sent to solitary in Pelican Bay for the remainder of their lives.

They had a Panamanian trainee pilot with them but this didn't stop them expressing their contempt for the Panamanians and a lack of faith in their ability to run the canal once it was handed over. The sailor who was highly anti-American whispered in my ear as he went off the bridge after handing over the wheel to another sailor, "They bumped off the previous Panamanian President you know. Carter signed a treaty with them which the Americans came to believe was too soft on the Panamanians and then this general refused to change it once Reagan came to power. They bumped him off.

General Omar Torrijos." He leaned in. "Look it up," he said. One of the Americans gave us a filthy look. I think he'd overheard.

The Panamanian pilot was to sit out on deck at the side of the ship and radio distances up to the American pilot on the bridge. He began to make a big fuss about shelters. "I can't stay out in the sun," he said. It might be considered a racist observation but he was as black as the ace of spades, so I found this a bit amusing. The American pilot started to lay into the captain about these shelters. The captain said that the ship didn't have any, but the American just continued going on and on about it. "Listen pilot, I can't f*****g give you what I haven't f*****g got," said the captain. The second mate winced. I suppressed a giggle. The American was astonished. He was clearly used to dealing with cowering third-world captains. This blunt-speaking Yorkshireman was different. I was quite confident the Captain could have laid both of these American pilots out if it came to a fight.

The American recoiled, but then a deal was quickly done. We would buy some shelters for an extortionate price from the canal authorities.

The captain was taking a risk. These American canal pilots were known to make it difficult for captains who'd given them gyp, when they came back the next time. Whether this authority is still abused now that the Panamanians are in charge, I don't know. I doubt it. I think it was an American attitude.

They didn't always win though. A friend had been through on a Shell ship and told me the pilot had said to the British captain, "Who do you think you are?" when the captain had failed to go scurrying to do as he was told. "I'm the captain," had said the captain, according to my friend, "the real one, not a part-time one who comes on board for five minutes." "We'll see how you get on next time," the pilot had apparently said. "Try it, just try and mess with Shell," the captain had supposedly told him. My friend had said that the pilot blanched. These oil companies carried a lot of power.

We entered the canal. The transit was an experience. The sailors didn't particularly like it though: it was a lot of work, as you were continually tying up and letting go the ropes as the ship moved through the locks.

The American pilots were taking turns on the bridge and I led the off-duty one down to a spare cabin. They were only on board for about twelve hours but they still required a cabin, so that the one whose turn it wasn't could have a lie-down. I opened the door for him and he turned on me and indignantly demanded to know what I thought this was. I looked through the door. It wasn't glamorous but it wasn't any worse than any of the other cabins on board. What was he expecting, a Cunard passenger suite.

"This is the cabin I was told to bring you to," I told him.

"And what happens if the other pilot has a heart attack?" he demanded. "I should be in a cabin next to the bridge." I thought about responding that maybe the captain could look after things for a minute or two, but he shoved me out of the way and went inside and slammed the door

I went up to the bridge. The second mate

was doing something at the chart table so I said quietly to him, "The pilot is not happy with his cabin." The second mate looked at me.

"What's wrong with it?" he said.

"It's not near enough to the bridge," I replied. He shook his head.

"American pilots," he said. "We could have given him the owner's cabin, I suppose. Never mind."

We continued on our way through the system.

The on-duty pilot soon slammed the ship into the side of a lock. His face twisted in fury, and the captain went and wrote something in the deck log. "That could cause a lot of damage," the sailor on the wheel whispered to me.

I was stuck inside a lot of the time but I managed to get out onto the bridge wings sometimes and observed the goings on, the workers tossing up the heaving lines and the little electric donkeys assisting us in moving along.

Half way through and I was sent down to wake the other pilot. I knocked on the cabin door. He shouted something. "Eh, your colleague says it's time to come up now," I said.

I went back up to the bridge and, after a while, the pilot burst in, a furious expression on his face. "Who knocked on my door?" he demanded, aggressively. I didn't answer. "Who knocked on my door!" he repeated more loudly.

"I did," I said.

"You're lucky I don't knock your teeth out," he shouted. "You woke me up for watch like that on a ship on which I was signed on and I'd break your jaw." I looked at the captain.

He just sighed. I think he was thinking, we'll get rid of them soon. These guys were supposed to be professionals. What did the pilot want me to do, wake him up with a little silver tray with some buttered toast and a cup of tea.

I took the other pilot down to the cabin and received the same complaints about it being too far from the bridge.

Eventually, we made it to Balboa, the small lake at the Pacific end. Suddenly, there was a loud crack.

At this time, General Noriega had decided that he wasn't happy with his redundancy cheque from the C.I.A. and the Bush family was getting worried about its property developments in Panama and the U.S. marines had been sent in to kick him out and were shooting the place up. I thought we were under fire and only just managed to stop myself diving onto the bridge floor. Then torrential rain hit us. It was just a tropical thunderstorm.

The captain came in from the bridge wing, soaked through. "Sometimes this job is overrated," he said to the pilot. The pilot laughed. They liked the captain; he'd stood up to them.

We entered the Pacific Ocean and the pilots left us. I was given the job of escorting them down to the main-deck accommodation ladder from which they'd board their pilot boat. On the way out, we passed the bosun. In a rare display of amity, he said, "How's it going, Willy?"

"Fine," I said, with a smile.

"Get a move on," said one of the pilots.

I thought about giving them two fingers once they were on their boat, but they'd probably put in a formal complaint.

The chief engineer rang the bridge and said, "We need to do some repairs," and the captain and second mate took the ship over to the outer anchorage. I quietly enquired as to how they were working out they were in the right spot and the second mate turned on me and insinuated that I was stupid. I slipped away.

Soon, we were able to limp along again. We now faced a thirty-five-day voyage to Yokohama.

The Pacific

The officers were now able to devote themselves more to winding-up the cadets.

There were two third engineers: one a, rail-thin, young Englishman who'd suffered from tuberculosis, and the other a vicious, nasty, little Scot.

The English one took me aside. "Do you know how to kill someone you don't like?" he said. I looked at him in bafflement. He leaned in. "A chipping hammer," he said. "The best technique is to wait for your victim to leave the ship's bar, then you creep up behind him and slam the point into his skull. Make sure you keep it vertical though or it'll just slip off and won't penetrate. Then you've got to get the body over the side. If you need someone to help you, be careful whom you ask and organise it in advance?"

I waited for him to laugh and say, I'm only joking. He didn't.

I'm still not sure he was joking. On the next tanker I was on there was a mate whom a sailor had actually tried to kill when the mate had been a teenage cadet, by slamming the point of a chipping hammer into his head. They'd found him on his blood-soaked bed when they went to wake him for his watch. He was a nice guy, but I don't think he had ever truly recovered. The company had merely sent his assailant home early. I think it would have been difficult to prove that he was the culprit, but apparently the company hadn't been all that bothered. It had happened during the mate's employment with a different company, not ours, but even so. He would fly off the handle sometimes. He tried to strangle me once after I'd stupidly made a flippant remark, but the engineers pulled him off me, with difficulty.

While on the subject of on-board violence, I was on one of the landings once and I noticed the captain walking around collecting all the fire axes. "What's he doing?" I asked the second mate.

"Oh, on one of our other ships, the sailors got drunk and decided they were going to use the fire axes to break into the bonded store, and, when the captain and the mates went down to deal with it, the sailors threatened to kill them," he said.

I thought of all the pretty recruitment brochures from the Chamber of Shipping featuring smiling cadets in nice uniforms (we wore orange boiler suits) posing with sextants while their cruise ships sailed under the Golden Gate Bridge. In my opinion, they should be prosecuted for misleading advertising.

Actually, I'm of the opinion that it'd be a lot better if Warsash scrapped all the firefighting and life raft induction training and replaced it with a month's intensive judo and boxing. The firefighting was mostly a waste of time anyway. Once these tankers were on fire, you were done for. And the life raft training was a waste of time, too. The life rafts were just there as a feel-good factor. Trying to get into them in rough seas from these huge ships would be nearly impossible, and if you were on a bulk carrier which spilt and went down, you had about five seconds after the split before it disappeared beneath the waves. But then IMO couldn't have endless standards and schedules about boxing and judo such as they had for all this safety training.

I wanted to get on with some training on board but there was a curious attitude to the cadetship training system. It was largely about sea time. Really, chipping paint and humping things around in the middle of the ocean wasn't particularly useful training, but the authorities only required that six months of your training was spent on the bridge. Even then, virtually all of that time could be spent in the middle of the Pacific. The whole system, in fact, was faulty.

From a learning point of view, it would have been a lot better if the authorities had insisted that some part of the training was spent on smaller ships trading in busier waters such as the North Sea. There is no room for daydreaming there. Fierce concentration is required and attention to the rules of the road at all times. I found in my time that the M.C.A. (Marine and Coastguard Agency) examiners seemed to look down on the coastal trade, maybe because they were often deep-sea men, themselves. They were reluctant to issue unlimited tickets if candidates hadn't a satisfactory amount of deep-sea time but what was the advantage to be gained from extra deep-sea time: days on end spent staring at a big blue semi-circle. Incidentally, another annoyance was that sometimes, if they didn't feel that you showed enough knowledge of some type of ship which you hadn't been on, they would offer you the option of your ticket being restricted to the type of vessel on which you had been working, or returning for re-examination later, perhaps after sometime on other types of ships, without a refund of your exam fee of course, but they would never restrict cruise ship peoples' tickets to cruise ships. I'm quite sure that P and O would have brought unsustainable pressure to bear on them if they'd tried it, but pure cruise ship cadets obviously hadn't served any time at all on any sort of cargo ships. I thought it was quite unfair.

The other cadet was looking a bit depressed. He'd wanted to be a policeman and been told by the Metropolitan Police that he was too young for them. "Why didn't you try one of the other police forces?" I'd asked him. "I want to be in the Met," he'd replied. Now he found himself on a tanker. He didn't really know why he'd applied. He would have been better off, if he wanted to be in the Met, to get some shoreside job and continually apply until the Metropolitan Police decided he was old enough and mature enough for them.

    We spent every morning carrying out soundings. This consisted of dropping a brass rod on a rope down pipes to the bottom of all the void spaces on the ship. This was a job which the Scandinavians had done once a year. The mate had us doing it daily. It took ages. He was quite right to insist on this, though. If the hull had rusted through and we were taking in water, we needed to know about it fast, but it was a monotonous job. The only highlight was that eventually we would wind up in the forecastle store where we could have a little natter, but then the vicious, little Scottish third engineer caught us loafing and immediately reported us to the mate. When we entered the cargo room with the soundings book, he turned on us. Halfway through berating us, he looked at the other cadet. "Why are you so miserable?" he demanded.

"All we ever do is soundings and chip paint?" he said.

"I know all you ever do is do soundings," replied the mate. "It takes you both forever." He sighed. "All right, you can do the lifeboats," he said.

The lifeboats were the third mate's responsibility, and so we were working under him.

It was a strange thing about the working hours that the mates were expected to do their eight hours on the bridge and two hours on deck every day while the sailors were only expected to work either eight hours of watches or do daywork. So, the mates, who were supposed to be senior to the sailors, were working more hours. I never understood this. The mate himself worked the four to eight watch in the morning, from eight to four on deck and then the four to eight watch in the evening, sixteen hours a day. And he got paid what a decent receptionist should expect in London. Might be sexist to suggest that he should be paid more than some girl answering the phone and painting her nails in the West End, but if you follow that line that everyone is essential so should be paid the same, you wind up with Soviet communism.

The third mate took us into the lifeboats. It was the first time we'd been in them. It wasn't a good idea to climb into them if you weren't told to, and have a look around. If you fell over the side, no one would know you'd suddenly disappeared from them. They might think you were in your cabin. There was a slim chance that if you went over the side and the ship's staff realised soon enough and turned the boat onto its reciprocal course and the sea was calm, you could be found. If it weren't noticed that you were missing, for even a little while, you were gone and that was that.

The Scandinavians had left the lifeboats complete wrecks. This was an old tanker and it had open lifeboats. I actually thought they were a better option than the newer ones. All right; they could get swamped unlike the newer, enclosed lifeboats but, if you could launch them while sinking, admittedly a big if, there was the possibility you could sail to safety. With the enclosed ones, you had to sit there and hope someone found you.

IMO was actually making safety at sea a problem right at this moment. They were doing away with radio officers. Under the radio officer system, every deep-sea ship and most coastal ships had a radio officer on duty for eight hours a day and for set times each hour he was listening on emergency shipping frequencies for distress signals. Under the new system, ships had a little satellite transmitter that sent a signal up to a satellite which eventually made its way to Stavanger in Norway. Stavanger in Norway would then try to initiate a rescue. Of course, there were too many variables now. The old system was better. A ship passing not too far away heard the S.O.S, altered course, and saved you. Now everything was done long distance. And IMO issued a requirement that the satellite alarms were tested. A lot of people didn't really know what they were doing, although there were courses being introduced, and half the deck officers who'd suddenly been informed that they were taking over the duties of the radio officers tested their devices by pressing the transmit button, thereby flooding Norway with thousands of false alarms. There had to be a further delay while alerts were verified otherwise every ship in the world would have been sent driving round in circles, attending non-existent emergencies. At best, I suppose, all this could be classified as the law of unintended consequences. At worst, it was simply a cost-saving exercise to benefit shipowners and no one was really bothered about ships sinking without anyone coming to their aide. Shipping companies were usually so over the moon to receive nice insurance cheques for their worn-out, old tonnage that a bit of compensation paid out to the families of some crew at the same time could be easily borne.

The third mate was good to work with. Being from the West County, he was into sailing and spicing bits of rope and all that. A sailor who'd done his training on general cargo ships with Harrisons of the Clyde helped us with making the wire strops. It was a difficult job, needing a lot of skill. Nowadays, you can't just make your own lifting strops and install them. Everything has to be properly tested and have a certificate. This gives employment to more shoreside companies and gives the endless procession of flag state and classification society inspectors something else to tick off on their little checklists.

The lifeboats had looked like they'd been abandoned on a seashore when we'd started. They looked like new by the time we'd finished, a month later.

To be fair to the Scandinavians, they weren't in the worst condition of any lifeboats I came across. I joined a British-run company as third mate years later and went into one of the lifeboats and moved the tiller and the last piece of rust holding the rudder on disintegrated and the rudder clattered onto the main deck.

There was a modicum of excitement in the air. It was soon going to be Christmas. It might seem pointless celebrating Christmas in the middle of the ocean: how could the day be any different, but the captain was determined to make an effort.

Christmas Eve was an early knock-off. We cadets got dragged into the crew bar and invited to a game of Trivial Pursuit. I didn't want to join in.

"Why not?" they demanded.

"I'm too good," I said. "You'll all want to kick my head in if I win too easily."

"So, you're a big head," said the nastiest one, the one from the strip club scenario, with the long string of G.B.H. convictions.

"It's not that. All I ever do is read books," I explained.

"Sit down and join in," said the bosun.

After ten minutes, we cadets had five pieces of cheese and they had none.

"You've been sitting up and reading the cards," said the vicious deckhand.

"Why would I bother to do that?" I demanded, exasperated. "I didn't even want to play anyway and I didn't even know we were going to be playing." Of course, I could have just deliberately got the answers wrong. I had tried that in similar situations, but I had too honest a face and it gave me away, and then people took offence at the implication that I was of the opinion that they were little children who had to be allowed to win.

Our last piece of cheese slipped into our holder and then the third mate appeared at the door of the crew messroom. "The mate wants to see you two," he said. I looked up at the sailors. They were staring at me. "Perhaps we'd better abandon this game," I suggested.

We followed the third mate out and up to the mate's cabin. "What are you doing in there with the crew?" he demanded.

"I don't know," I told him. "They wanted us to play Trivial Pursuit. I didn't want to. They insisted."

"You shouldn't go in there," he said. "You don't come into the officers' bar. You don't want to socialise with us. Why do you want to go into the crew bar?"

"I don't want to," I replied. "I stay out of the officers' bar because I find in any argument that I'm always in a minority of one, so it's best not to be in there."

We had been in there once and I'd found that the officers practised a kind of verbal judo. They would ask a question which had to be answered with a very definite answer one way or the other. Whichever you opted for, they would immediately take offence. Just staying quiet or declining to get into disputes wasn't tolerated.

In their defence, I suppose, the crew did the same.

"Get in the officers' bar," said the mate. I knew what was going to be next. The sailors would start being all offended that we wanted to drink with the officers, not with them. If we protested that the mate had insisted we did this, they wouldn't want to listen.

We went into the officers' bar and sat on some stools. The captain was glaring at us. The second engineer, a huge, ginger-bearded Scotsman nicknamed the Honey Monster, put a beer in front of each of us.

"Nah," said the captain and he pulled out of the freezer compartment of the fridge a bottle of some horrible spirit which the Scandinavians had left on board and tipped some into two shot glasses and handed them to us. This stuff was literally potentially lethal. We'd have been better off drinking the cargo. The second engineer tried to protest but the captain signaled that he should shut up.

The other cadet tipped his back obligingly. He looked like he was in shock, and then his face turned bright red. A few moments later, he stood up, wobbled, and then went out of the door.

"Follow him and see if he's all right," said the second engineer. I slipped off my stool and exited the bar.

Along the corridor, I saw the other cadet paused at the top of the staircase. "All right?" I asked him.

He turned to look at me and then fell head first down the stairs. In horror, I rushed along the corridor and down the staircase and found him bleeding heavily from his forehead.

Suddenly, all the others were around me. "Did you push him?" asked the tuberculosis-victim third engineer.

"Why would I push him?" I said. "You lot just poisoned him, and he fell over." This was typical. They were trying to blame me, probably covering themselves in case he was badly hurt and they had to make a report to the office.

The captain took him away to the ship's hospital to bandage him up.

We were lucky with our medical services. Normally, only the mate and the captain had Ship Captains' Medical Certificates. Most captains and mates; however, didn't want to get involved with medical treatment anymore because of all the hysteria about HIV. Since that came in, they'd been insisting that the second and third mates, who normally didn't have these certificates, attended to all the medical emergencies. Our captain and chief mate weren't like that.

For really big emergencies, you were supposed to use radio medical advice. This was usually provided by The Royal Naval hospital at Haslar. However, I was on a ship which had had Korean crew and the captain had been receiving instructions for the treatment of a Korean A.B. who'd smashed his head open, falling from a hatch, and the Royal Navy doctor had suddenly realised the crew member concerned wasn't British. "Give him an aspirin and send him to bed," he'd said and then hung up. The same company had had another incident in U.S. waters in which a second engineer had been seriously ill. "Has he been drinking?" the U.S. Doctor had asked. The ship's officers had thought about this. It was illegal to have been drinking in U.S. waters so they said that he hadn't. Unfortunately, the doctor then prescribed drugs from the ship's medical locker which, when combined with alcohol, were likely to kill the patient. It was only due to the fact that the second engineer was so fat and blubbery that the medicine wasn't sufficient to kill him.

Festivities resumed half an hour later, the other cadet sitting at the bar with only a beer in front of him now and his head all bandaged up. No one insisted that I drank my glass of evil spirit.

There was another Trivial Pursuit box in the officers' bar and they decided we should play a game. I didn't want to but, having already been labelled unsociable, I didn't say anything.

I was put on the captain's side. Almost the first question was, which is the biggest country solely in the southern hemisphere. I said, "Australia." The captain said, "Brazil." If I'd known he thought it was Brazil, I would have kept quiet. He overruled me and then seemed to insist that I join him in his opinion and our joint answer was Brazil.

The second mate, who was on the other side, smiled. "It's Australia," he said. He ridiculed the captain. "Brazil goes to five north," he said. The captain was fuming. I'd embarrassed him. This whole afternoon was a disaster.

The next day was Christmas Day, more drinkies and a round of present giving. The presents weren't from the company; the company didn't care about us. They were from the seamen's mission in Houston. Families spent the year making up little Christmas boxes and giving them to the mission to donate to ships I was touched by this. I thought it was a really nice gesture. Some of the American politicians and businessmen might be evil, but some of the normal people are genuinely nice human beings.

Some of the boxes had little letters in them and you could write to the families and say 'thank you'. Sadly, mine didn't.

I got a nice pair of socks and some other bits and pieces.

Later on, we went down for our Christmas dinner. The cook had made a bit of an effort and it was good. It was the only time that the crew and the officers ate together. The vicious A.B. with the string of G.B.H. convictions didn't come in. He'd had a dispute with the captain on another ship on which the captain had been the mate, and he was still brooding about it.

The second mate stayed up on the bridge, until the captain went up to relieve him.

A week went by and then we went through the whole rigmarole for New Year's.

On New Year's morning, the other cadet looked a bit discontented. "What's wrong?" I said.

"They carried the second mate up to do his watch last night," he said.

"So?" I replied. He just mumbled.

It was quite British, I thought, that the captain would get extremely upset about some minor breech of etiquette, but things like this didn't seem to bother him, though, to be fair, he was forever trying to get the second mate to go to bed in the evenings instead of staying in the bar. But he liked the second mate, and the second mate was his protégé. When I became a captain, I found it was very difficult to discipline one's protégés. You naturally wanted to protect them.

The festivities over, we were sent out chipping and painting again, and then the weather began to turn.

I'd never realised that the sea could get this bad. We were stuck on the bridge as it became too dangerous to work out on deck. The second mate would look up from his chart table whenever we hit a particularly big one and ask us to go round the front and check that the bow hadn't fallen off. The first time he said this, we thought he was joking.

"I'm not joking," he'd said. "It happens on ships like this." What did he mean by that, I thought: old and rusty ones or ships of this design.

We went round and confirmed that the bow was still attached.

"Good," said the second mate.

"Will we have time to get into the lifeboats if the bow does fall off?" I asked.

"Possibly," he said. He was virtually imperturbable. I'd only seen him fired up once and that was when he lost his temper with me at Panama. He was only twenty-five and had been at sea ten years. Imagine someone ashore being so mature and unflappable at such an early age, and having such life experience.

It'd taken its toll on him physically, though. His face looked like that of a forty year old and he had a pot belly. He wanted to leave and become a fireman but I didn't think that there was any way he'd ever pass the fitness tests.

The spell of bad weather was soon over and we were back to being in the middle of a flat blue disc and us cadets and the sailors were sent out on deck again.

The first job I did was with the mate. He had to tighten some piece of machinery. We went down a hatch from the forecastle store and climbed all the way to the bottom of the ship. It was dark, dank and dangerous. I wondered about all those safety regulations. We hadn't followed any of them. There were no rescue teams at the top. We weren't wearing escape sets. We had them on board but it was thought a bit gay to wear them. The chief mate didn't seem bothered by the danger.

I just passed him rags and tools. After a while, he was satisfied. "See her to the scrapyard," he said. Without thinking, I quipped, "Another six months?" The chief mate did not have a sense of humour and Merchant Navy officers took anything which impugned their professionalism very seriously. "She'll last longer than you will," he said. I wanted to explain that I was only making a joke about the ship, not his work, but I thought better of it. I fell silent. I wondered what he meant. Was I likely to be murdered, or was he thinking of firing me, or did he expect me to have an accident.

I'd almost killed myself once, already. I'd been told to throw a piece of junk steel over the side and had done so and just as I let go, I realised that I was standing in a coil of rope which was attached to it. If it had tightened up on my foot, the weight of the steel might have been more than I could hold, clinging on to the rail, and I might have followed it over the side. I just managed to whip my foot clear in time.

After this job at the bottom of the ship, the mate had me join the other cadet in repainting the tank valves. The boat was sort of semi-manual. You had to go out on deck to open and close tank valves, but they were hydraulically powered. The newer ships could be completely controlled from the cargo room; the older ones had only manual valves and not even a control room.

Over time, bits of pieces of the valves had got mixed up and the colour-coding was all wrong.

This wasn't such a bad job, sitting on deck, painting the valve spokes the right colours.

The mate took all the valves and their associated hydraulics off, one by one, and wheeled them to the workshop and repaired them, fixing all the leaks. Why the Scandinavians couldn't have done this in the years they'd had the boat, I didn't know.

The mate was a machine. He never tired. I thought we should be helping him, but then he was quite skillful, and we'd have probably spent more time getting in his way than helping.

It was strange, but on tankers the mates were expected to perform all this mechanical work out on deck and yet they had no mechanical training. You would have thought it would be the engineers' job but the engineers' responsibility stopped at the engine-room bulkhead. They wouldn't even do the plumbing because in the old days either the ship's carpenter did that or they had a deck fitter and then, when these staff were taken away, as they had been, the responsibility for this job had remained with the deck department and the mates had ended up with it.

I thought it was unfair that the engineers wouldn't help outside, but they didn't care what anyone thought of them, certainly not a deck cadet, and I kept my mouth firmly shut in front of them. If I hadn't, I would have got a fist in the face.

They were odd too in another way. They were on daywork and highly reluctant to leave the engine room between eight and five, other than for lunch. They even resented having to attend lifeboat drills. However, at one minute after five, you wouldn't find any of them down there.

I mentioned some of these observations to the second mate. "Aha," he said, "oil and water. You're going to fit right in if you're already developing that attitude to the engineers."

The sailors left us alone with our painting, and I was glad not to be working with them for a while. They were always sending us running around when we did, which was all right, but they were forever doing their 'taking offence' act. One would send one of us in to see if another was in the crew messroom and then whoever was in the crew messroom would be offended that we were constantly sticking our heads in, looking around for someone and then diving out again.

We settled into our routine. In order to avoid further allegations that we were unsociable, we started to go into the officers' bar a bit more. Then the happy mood in there was suddenly gone because the engineers had a massive dispute among themselves.

The chief engineer had decided that the other engineers were skiving and given them a big ticking off. They had not taken this well and were fighting back. The second engineer was the most offended, the tuberculosis-victim third engineer supporting him.

Years later, I was to sail with a mate who'd sailed with this second engineer when he was first promoted. This mate had claimed that when the company's superintendent (it was a different company) had come on board, he'd been so annoyed by the state of the engine room that he'd tried to fire this second engineer. The only thing that saved him was that his family had Freemasonry connections and that the superintendent on board was only looking after that boat for a different superintendent for a little while and couldn't fire him without the approval of the ship's regular superintendent. So, maybe there was something in the chief engineer's allegations, but I didn't know what state the engine room was supposed to be in or whether or not they were working efficiently,

I thought the captain would get in the middle and calm it down but he didn't seem to want to be involved. I wondered if the tuberculosis-victim third engineer, who'd so enthusiastically offered his murder schemes, was going to try to kill the chief.

I liked all the engineers apart from the nasty, little, Scottish third. I didn't understand why they couldn't get on.

It was convenient for us because every night, just as the argument was firing up again, either the second engineer or the chief engineer would turn round and say, "I'm not continuing this conversation in front of cadets," and we would get thrown out of the bar; thus appearing to want to be sociable and at the same time escaping being stuck in there with them. While all this went on, we just sort of had to turn up at the beginning of the sessions as a formality.

I started going up to the bridge to spend time with the third mate on his eight to twelve watch in the evening. He was a strange character: jolly, one minute, ranting the next. It was essential to keep him off the subject of the Jews as he was so irrational about them.

On other things, he was quite fun and very informative. He alerted me about the Freemasonry aspect of the Merchant Navy. I didn't listen to him, however, when it came to his advice about which companies were hotbeds of Freemasonry and should be avoided; and when I had my ticket, I would go to work for two of them. I never got invited to join, though. I wouldn't have done anyway as my family had had a bad experience at their hands.

One thing I noticed was that the deck officers could talk about things other than the ship; the engineers could only really hold a conversation on the subject of the engine. As soon as the conversation drifted away from that subject, you would see them itching to get it back on, what they considered to be, track.

The junior mates were dreamers. You had to be to do that job, just staring out at a blue circle. As with every job, computers were taking the skill out of bridge watchkeeping. GPS hadn't yet come in but they had another, not so good, system which gave you a position every few hours and they had radars and plotting aids.

Paradoxically, however, though the bridge watchkeeping had become simpler, the deck operations had got more complicated. This was a fairly low-tech tanker, but some of the newer ones were incredibly difficult. It always seemed to me mad that the mates were running all this equipment. For doing that, you needed technically-minded people. The mates weren't technically minded. The companies answer had been to start taking on A-level cadets, in the days when A-Levels meant something, and training them up. But then you ended up with brainy people like the chief officer (the mate) who were bored stiff on the bridge and started to look around for a shore job after a few years.

There was no solution really. You couldn't very well insist that all the electronics on the bridge were junked so that the mates had something to stretch their minds; they were becoming mandatory. You couldn't insist that ships were manual; the companies were further reducing the crews.

This division between the newer, brainier types and the, old, romantic, daydreamer types was well represented by the contrast between the chief mate and the third mate. The third mate resented the chief mate. The chief mate was forever telling him he was, "Not using his time properly." The third mate said the chief mate was round the twist and had been driven round the twist by being too brainy. The second mate thought the chief mate was officious and the third mate was incompetent. Trying to work out who loathed whom and why was like trying to unravel a big ball of string. It's easy to think you should just stay out of it, then, but they were constantly bringing you in.

Japan

Thirty-five days out from Panama and we were approaching Japan. The ship's staff began to move into a higher gear. The mate became a little manic.

I went down to the ship's ladder to meet the pilot. The other cadet and one of the sailors were in the middle of a little conflict. The pilot ladder had had to be lowered a little bit and the cadet had gone and got one of the sailors to do it, who'd told him he should have been able to do it himself. They were both right, really. On the one hand, the cadet was one of that type of people who always tries to avoid doing anything on the basis that if you never take responsibility for anything, you can never be blamed, and, on the other hand, the sailor should have done it because he was more experienced and there was a very high rate of accidents during pilot boarding.

The Japanese pilots appeared, and looked in mystification at this evidence of disharmony in front of them.

I was quite surprised by their ages. The senior pilot looked to be about ninety and his apprentice looked to be about eighty. "Lift?" said the senior one.

"No lift," I replied.

I led them up through the inside. They were both panting. I was seriously worried that they'd have heart attacks. Why were the

Japanese authorities employing such elderly staff.

The captain greeted them, and I went over to the chart table and made the relevant entry in the deck log.

The ship's electrician appeared. Everyone hated him because he was so selfish and a moaner but there was sometimes no avoiding him.

"In the early seventies, this bay was full of ships," he said. I looked out of the window. It was pretty packed now. "Full," he said with emphasis. "And now look." He peered over the chart table at the pilots. "First time I came here," he said, "the pilot dinged the ship and he was mortified. The captain was going, "It's all right, pilot, I don't care, it's dented anyway," and then the pilot apologised, went down onto the quay, and committed suicide." It sounded an unlikely story to me, but he insisted it was true. He went away.

I was sent down to help make the tug fast.

Tying up tugs and mooring was difficult. We cadets weren't as strong as the sailors and we'd be pulling on these huge ropes and hardly shifting them and the sailors would tear them out of our hands and whip them across the deck and swear at us. You needed muscles.

The ropes were not the dangerous aspect though, that was the wire springs. The springs did a lot of the work. They were what really held the boat. They were on winches, luckily; we didn't have to take them on and off the drum end and make them up on the bitts, but they were still dangerous. The B.P. guys were always going on about an accident that they said had happened on one of their ships years ago. The ship had come out new from a British shipyard, but the shipbuilders had only tack-welded the dollies, the upright pillars with spinning heads around which the wires were guided. One had snapped off and the wire had taken the legs off two men. That was a freak accident, but wires were always snapping.

I sailed with someone later on who'd seen a guy decapitated right in front of him. There was a postscript to this story. The captain had rung his company to inform them, and the company official had said, "Was he wearing his safety boots?" The captain had said, "What difference does that make; he was decapitated." "If he wasn't wearing his safety boots then he wasn't complying with our safety regulations and we don't have to pay his widow any compensation," the company official had replied.

This was the type of evil person you sometimes had running shipping companies now. The trouble was, things had switched over from shipping companies being owned and run by individuals and their families to shipping companies being owned and run by corporations. Once you got into the world of accountants and bankers, humanity was out of the window. I sailed with an old captain who'd come from Blue Funnel. He said he'd been up the offices once and the owner had told him, "Listen, I don't care if the company makes fifty million a year or fifty thousand. I can't spend even fifty thousand so it makes no difference to me." Of course, once professional finance people are in charge, that attitude is out.

We were finally tied up. We used fourteen

wires and ropes at each end of the boat.

The pilots went off and the refinery people came on board. They went in to see the mate and then went around the deck. They looked puzzled. "Chief," they said to the mate, "we can't believe this is the same ship. It has been coming here for years with the deck awash in hydraulic oil and now it's suddenly clean."

"I fixed it," said the mate. They nodded and went away. Half an hour later, they were back with a bottle of whiskey. "Well done, chief," they said, giving it to him.

I went away up to the manifold to help the sailors change the connections.

"How are the Japanese?" Asked the anti-American sailor.

"Fine," I said.

"You'd think they wouldn't be," he continued. I looked at him with puzzlement.

"Why?" I asked.

"After what the Americans did to them," he said. When I continued to not understand, he looked at me as if I were stupid. "Hiroshima," he said. "They burnt the skin off women and little children, hundreds of thousands of them."

"Yeah, but they said they would have lost a million men if they'd had to invade," I replied.

"MacArthur had already negotiated the surrender," said the sailor. "Truman wanted to fulfil America's 'manifest destiny'. That's why he dropped the bomb, well two of them actually, despite the fact that the Japanese wanted to surrender. That's why he hated MacArthur: MacArthur knew too much."

"I thought 'manifest destiny' was all about wiping out the Indians," I said. These were the days before conspiracy theories were mainstream and when people still believed that government had good intentions. This sailor just came across as mad.

"Nah," he said, "'manifest destiny' was about dropping the bomb." He walked off.

"They didn't even have the bomb when they came up with that," I said to him. It was to no avail. He wasn't listening. I thought, I bet he didn't write all this on his U.S. Visa application.

Shortly after this, I nearly got punched out by the mate over something which wasn't really my fault. The other cadet came to me. "There's a problem," he said.

"What?" I demanded.

"The refinery's laid on a minibus out but there isn't one back in."

"So, it'll get sorted out," I replied.

"Can't you say something to the mate?"

"Why don't the sailors?" I asked him.

"They think you should, too," he said.

Great, I thought, they're gobby enough normally but they don't want to go and confront the mate.

"Why don't you do it?" I asked him.

"You're the oldest," he said.

I sighed. "Do we really want to go, anyway?" I said. "Think about it, six hours working, mad rush ashore for six hours, half of which we'll spend in the minibus, followed by six hours' working, followed by six hours off-duty."

"Go on," he said.

I went into the cargo room where the mate was sat at his desk while the refinery people did some calculations. I explained the problem. "You can go ashore if you're off watch," he said. "But," I replied, "it's a bit mad isn't it, if we can't get back into the refinery." He suddenly flew out of his chair, pushed me out of the cargo room onto the deck and slammed me up against the bulkhead.

"You're trying to embarrass me in front of the refinery staff," he said. "You're lucky I don't knock your teeth out," etc... etc... Out of the corner of my eye, I saw the other cadet turn around and walk away up the deck.

"I'm only mentioning it," I gasped, choking. He threw me away from him. "Get back to work," he said. You had to be careful with these guys. They were all volatile.

Great, I thought, I didn't even care if we went and now I'd received all the blame for the moaning.

After the mate had finished with the refinery people, he went up to see the captain and the minibus was organized more efficiently.

Yokohama was not very welcoming. We weren't allowed into ninety per-cent of the bars. One of the sailors would approach the doorman and then come back laughing. "No round-eyes," he would say. The Japanese are very nice and efficient but they are the most racist people on the planet. But then, I thought, you're running your nice little peaceful bar, do you really want a gang of British hooligans piling in.

We finally found one that would tolerate our custom and went upstairs to the karaoke lounge. I'd never heard of karaoke. It hadn't arrived in Britain yet. When I returned to Britain, I would be saying, "This karaoke thing is going to come here and be massive." "What are you talking about?" People would say to me. "Singing along to backing tracks in the pub. No one wants to do that."

The steward turned out to be the best singer. Even the Japanese liked his singing. They soon had him doing Sinatra numbers.

He had a way with the ladies. He had wavy blonde hair and blue eyes and a laid-back manner. A couple of slinky Japanese girls were soon perched on the wings of his armchair.

After this, we went to a restaurant. It had a round, spinning table and this almost caused a fight. There was one huge prawn left and just as one of the sailors was about to spear it with his fork, another one spun the table and ate it.

The others calmed things down and we went outside and waited for the minibus back to the refinery.

One of them found a beer dispensing machine along the street. I tried to imagine such a thing in the street in the U.K. How long would it last. Not even ten minutes, I think.

Soon, I was on the ship and out on deck and working. I was quite tired which was my own fault for going up the road. The thinking behind Merchant Navy administration nowadays is that you write off a few months of your life when you join a ship and live it up while on leave. The old days of there being life on a ship and ships having regular ports where the sailors all had regular ladies was just about on its last legs. Some of the boys on the induction course had gone off to Blue Star which was just about hanging on, but working on their ships was just about the only remnant of the traditional Merchant Navy life.

I wasn't sure that all this progress was good. Even then, a container ship could carry what five general cargo ships could have carried, with a fifth of the crew. The newer giant container ships can take far more. Who gained from all this? The company shareholders? But all the potential dividends would be ripped off by City pension fund administrators before it ever reached the pensioners. The crews certainly weren't paid more. The population at home got to buy cheap rubbish that it didn't need and wouldn't even want if it weren't bombarded with advertising. But what was the alternative. If you didn't stick with working on ships, what were you going to do: be one of those City crooks, ripping off widows' and orphans' pension funds, become a lawyer twisting the law to keep criminals out of prison or slinging have-a-go heroes simply trying to defend their properties and families into jail. It was difficult.

I knew more about the cargo system now and like to think I became more of a help than a hindrance. I was still on watch with the third mate. Mindful of the constant complaints from the second mate, I tried to make sure that the tanks levels were better organised.

This time, of course, we were discharging. This was more interesting than loading.

The cargo flowed out along the pipes at the bottom of the ship, through the ship's four huge pumps, along the pipes on top of the deck and then out through the manifold to the refinery.

As the tanks reached the lowest level at which the big pumps could maintain suction, we used a stripping pump. This operation involved a lot of peering through butterworth holes at the bottom of the tanks with a torch. This wasn't a particularly pleasant operation.

Imagine sticking your face over the filler opening in your car's petrol tank, breathing in all the fumes, while trying to look down it with a penlight. It was important, though. The more cargo left, the bigger the problem with the figures and the more oil we'd be left to sort out once we cleaned the tanks.

After a few hours of discharging, we had a little fire. This was in the engine room. The mate donned a fire suit and breathing apparatus and went straight down there to find the engineers standing around a burnt-out piece of machinery with some fire extinguishers in their hands. The Japanese had looked at me while the alarms were going off and I had just shrugged. I hadn't left the deck. You weren't supposed to during cargo and I'd thought it was the lesser of two evils to not attend the fire alarm rather than to abandon my post, plus I didn't want to panic the Japanese. There would be plenty of people who knew what they were doing fighting the fire anyway.

They never told the Japanese there was a fire, not during, nor after; and we carried on discharging jet fuel. This was despite the reams and reams of checklists and codes of practices by which we were supposed to abide. If the whole ship had gone up, it would have taken out half of Yokohama. I mentioned this to one of the sailors, quietly, later on. "They should be used to it by now," was his dry observation. Such humor wouldn't be thought funny nowadays, but this was thirty years ago.

There was some postscript to this. Despite not having told the refinery, the ship did tell the company. It had to anyway or how would it explain the piece of machinery being burnt out. The third mate, who was the officers' safety representative on the safety committee, made a comment about the mate not waiting for the full support party to gather before he went charging down the engine room. The mate took great offence at this criticism. Opinion was divided among the sailors. On the one hand there were those who said, "Yep, he definitely violated the procedures," and on the other hand, there were those who said, "He did the right thing; if there's a fire, you don't stand around having little meetings, you do something about it."

As part of our studies, we were supposed to write little reports on our experiences and get them signed by the mate. I wrote one out on this incident and took it to him to sign. He wouldn't sign it. Officially, the reason was that it would open a whole can of worms at my oral examination for second mate's; unofficially, I thought he was still brooding on the third mate's justified or unjustified criticism. I'd actually written that he waited for the fire party, but, despite this, he still wouldn't sign it.

The other cadet was on watch with the second mate. He complained that while he was kneeling on the deck, checking a ballast tank's ullage with a tape and had keeled over asleep, the second mate had kicked him in the head in frustration. He didn't seem to be very marked. The second mate obviously hadn't kicked him very hard, because we wore steel toe-capped boots and the second mate would have split his skull if he'd kicked him with any force.

The mate was still alert, despite his hours. He truly was a machine. The third mate just sneered at him behind his back and called him 'Roadrunner' after the cartoon character, which was a bit unfair.

During cargo, the chief mate would often be working thirty-six hours straight. I found this strange. If someone were working thirty-six hours straight while in charge of an operation at a refinery, the authorities would go mad, but if it were on a ship, they didn't seem to mind.

The authorities could be quite hard on captains if someone on board made a mistake due to over-tiredness. They didn't mind slinging them in jail.

There was an incident in which a ship hit an oil rig. The captain had written to the company pointing out the excessive hours being worked but they didn't assist him with extra staff or easier schedules, and the mate fell asleep on the bridge and hit the oil rig. The authorities slung both of them in jail. They did not jail anyone from the company.

The companies also use the same psychology the military does. The military knows that men don't fight for their country or for their armies; they fight for their comrades. You are made to feel as if you're letting your colleagues down if you don't do that extra bit.

In another incident, a captain reported a deficiency in the safety equipment to the British authorities but, because he took the boat out, being under pressure, having only just joined, the authorities fined him. This was hardly going to encourage other captains to be whistle-blowers is it.

Another problem was that captains were losing their authority. They were keeping all the responsibility but the authority was passing on to the shoreside managers. To compound the problem, the shoreside managers with the power were no longer generally ex-captains who understood the problems, they were financial people. Captains sometimes had to spend ages justifying expenditures or explaining problems to managers who, if they had been ex-captains, wouldn't have needed any explanations.

This was a bit like Britain going forty years without a minister of defence who had any military experience.

Eventually, we'd stripped our tanks and were ready to set off for Singapore. Two different, ancient pilots came on board; the tugs surrounded the ship, and we were out. It was a shame we hadn't seen more of Japan.

"Get used to this," said the second mate. "Your shore time will be even less once you get your ticket."

"What's the answer?" I asked him.

"Ain't one," he replied.

I was surprised that the captain didn't get more involved with cargo and it was all left to the mate. The captain had told us once, when he was feeling sociable, that he'd had a terrible mate on his first trip in command and had had to do the whole job himself and now he was just grateful that he had a highly competent one whom he could leave alone to get on with the job. The second mate said, however, that the captain had been newly promoted when he'd sailed with that other mate and that all newly-promoted captains had a hard time leaving the mate's job to the mate; they always wanted to do it themselves, so maybe that mate hadn't been incompetent; maybe the captain just wouldn't leave him alone.

"So, what do you think?" said the mate to

us, first morning in the cargo room after we'd left Yokohama.

"We didn't get much time off," blurted out the other cadet. That was a mistake, I thought but the chief mate just laughed. "Get used to it," he said. "Once you've got your ticket, you can always go on some other type of ship. Neither of you is nasty enough to get a job in the office, though."

"Don't want to work in the office," said the other cadet.

"No, I understand that you want to be a policeman," said the mate. The other cadet blushed. "And you want to be a writer," the mate said to me. How did he know that. Now, I blushed. "You've got to have something to write about, though," he added, looking at me through narrowed eyes. He was a clever man.

"The captain likes you," one of the sailors had said to me, the youngest one who was only our age. "The mate doesn't particularly, but the captain does."

The captain seemed to hate the other cadet, which was a surprise as the other cadet was a fellow Yorkshireman. I wondered why he liked me and not him.

Then one day, the captain enlightened me. He was giving me a ticking off about some minor offence and I must have looked a bit despondent, because he suddenly said, "I can see you're keen; I'm not blind." I said nothing. "There's no way any of us can make it any easier for you on here. It is what is is," he continued. "You just have to like it or lump it. Do your tickets as quickly as you can and become a captain as quickly as you can. You'll be sailing with foreign junior officers because by then all the British junior officers will have been fired, but still, that's the best advice I can give you. Don't even think about going into the office."

The second mate was more cynical. "Become a City wheeler dealer or a lawyer," he said, "because they are the only two professions which the Government cares about."

Tank cleaning

Now we were about to embark upon the longest and most dangerous job on board, tank cleaning.

This job was quite difficult. Technically, if you were loading a coarser grade than the one which you had just discharged, you didn't need to do it but what surveyor was going to pass dirty tanks when he didn't have to, so it pretty much always had to be done between cargoes. The only time you might get away without doing it would be if you were on an oil-company-owned ship, carrying one of their own cargoes.

There were several steps. First the tanks had to be washed.

We had huge hoses on reels which we trundled around the deck. These had spinning nozzles attached to them. They were called butterworth machines. We would lower the hoses down the tanks, connect up the ends to the seawater line, and then open the valves and start the pump. After a little while, we would wind up the hoses and move on to the next tanks.

Then we had these bright yellow fan machines which we also trundled around the deck and placed over the butterworth holes. They were supposed to suck all the gases out of the tanks. There were figures for how many cubic metres of air they could change per hour, but there was always a feeling that we should get the job done as quickly as possible so the pressure was on. Really, gas-freeing wasn't a precise science and doing each tank for the minimum time wasn't a brilliant idea.

There were only a few of us to do this: the other cadet and myself, the bosun, the dayworker and whichever lookout was on duty.

After the tanks were gas free, they had to be checked. The mate wanted the second mate to do this but the second mate wouldn't. Really, the captain should have told the second mate to get his arse out on deck but he didn't. This was the one thing I didn't understand about the captain. He would never support his officers. The third mate had had a massive row with one of the sailors and the captain hadn't supported him. Apparently; the captain had been a bit of a rebel when he was a cadet and mate and maybe he found it difficult to see he should support the officers against other rebels. Anyway, the second mate finally, reluctantly, agreed to show me how to check the tanks. He briefly ran though the procedure at one tank and then disappeared again.

I was left with two detectors, a gas detector and an oxygen detector. I started to work my way around.

I found out a while later that there had been another argument while I was doing this. The mate had wanted the second mate to spend more time than he had showing me, but the second mate never came out on deck again, so I just had to get on with it.

I checked the tanks. It was ridiculous really. You just dropped the suction tubes down the tanks, sampling the atmosphere at three random levels. There could be pockets of gas all over the place and you wouldn't know.

Nevertheless, I did as I was told. I found one tank at which the gas reading was thirty-nine per cent. It was supposed to be less than two. I went into the cargo room and informed the mate. The mate came strutting out on deck with the other cadet following him. He flipped open the inspection hatch and sniffed. "That is not thirty-nine per-cent," he said. "I have a trained nose. I can tell." He dipped the tube and the needle flicked to exactly thirty-nine per-cent. He flushed with anger. "Well," he said. "That's why we test the tanks. Get the fans on it again."

Informing him like this might have been an error on my part. The mate would make me suffer for this. But how could I have avoided it. The tank had an explosive atmosphere and that was that. I suppose I should have found some more diplomatic way of passing on the information.

All the tanks were just under the borderline for going down them. In order to make them as gas-free and clean as possible, we'd have had to take much longer washing and gas-freeing them.

Now the highly dangerous work began, at the bottom of the tanks. We had to climb down these sixty-foot ladders, which in itself was dangerous, remove steel cover plates on suction holes on the pipework to the pumps, bolt on suction pipes, shout up that we were ready, and then once the pumps had been started, hoover up the washing dregs from the bottom of the tanks.

The atmosphere was horrible. It was more or less equivalent to getting inside a car's petrol tank after it had been swilled out.

Just to make it a little more dangerous, on top of the risk of being overcome by fumes, you had to walk along some treacherous stairways in the gloom with only the aid of dim torches, and, once you were on the bottom plates, step over stringers; and you risked slipping in the pools of water on top of which floated carcinogenic, oily filth.

It was supposed to be three minutes without air and you were brain damaged, four minutes and you were dead. There was no way they were going to get anyone out within four minutes, let alone three. Even fifteen would be pushing it.

The bosun took me down the first tank I was going to clean. "Jesus Christ," I exclaimed within moments. I had very nearly walked straight off the end of a walkway. It went along a few yards above the bottom of the tank and then just disappeared. There was a ladder leading down from it to the bottom of the tank but no railing to stop you walking straight off the end.

The bosun turned to see what the problem was. I was staring in horror at the opening. "Got to look where you're going, Willy," he said.

In some ways, it was beautiful down in the tanks, though. Some light came through the butterworth holes and was cast in circles as in that famous photograph of Grand Central Station. It was like being in a huge cavern.

While you were at the bottom of the tank, someone was supposed to be watching you from the top through one of the butterworth holes. Whenever I looked up, I couldn't see a face there. I suppose the mate was right. If you keeled over, you were brain damaged very soon and probably it would be best if they let you die rather than brought you up like that.

Warsash had pumped us full of all this safety gumpf. There was supposed to be a rescue team at the top, breathing apparatus at the ready etc.., But we were on minimum manning. If you followed all this, you would take months to clean all the tanks.

The minimum manning was an issue. We were an Isle of Man registered ship. The Isle of Man registry is extremely touchy about accusations that it's a flag of convenience, but I found out once that, at the time, a British flagged tanker would have required more crew. "Who's right?" I asked an Isle of Man surveyor whom I ran into. "The United Kingdom flag says one level of manning, you say another. Is the United Kingdom flag wrong about the safe manning level?" He wouldn't answer directly, but just kept repeating, "We evaluate a safe level of manning."

I waded around in the oily water, sucking it up through the pipe. I wondered how many cancer-inducing chemicals I was breathing in. It was quite incredible really that the authorities thought that this was a safe working procedure. Amusingly, later on, the other cadet and I were handed a pot of glue and some safety signs alerting users to the possibility of burning themselves with hot water from the mixer taps in the showers and told to stick one up in each cabin bathroom, it being a requirement of the Isle of Man flag. The authorities didn't mind us wandering around in these reeking tanks, but they were terrified that we'd be so stupid as to scald ourselves in our own showers.

It took a while to hoover up what you could and then it was down to scooping the last bit into buckets. Once a bucket was full, you would scream at the top of your voice, and eventually a face would appear over a butterworth hole, and then a sailor or the other cadet would haul your bucket of oily water up and tip it over the side.

I had one nasty incident, but it wasn't being gassed. The nastiest sailor, the one with the G.B.H. convictions, was sent down to relieve me just before I put the cover plate back on the suction pipe. I handed him the spanner and moved away and started climbing the ladder. Suddenly, he started shouting at me. I turned round. "What?" I said. "Where are the bolts?" he demanded. I pointed to them. They were on a little webbing plate right next to him "That's a stupid place to put them," he said. "Well, where else would I put them?" I asked. "Not there, that's a stupid place," he said. "It's no joke down here, you know." I knew it was no joke, I'd been down the tanks all morning. "Well you've got them now," I said. "There's some prats I have to work with on this ship," he shouted, and then he launched into a whole string of obscenities. I made my way to the top of the tank and out on deck.

I don't know if there was something in my facial expression, but the bosun said to me, "All right, Willy?" with a quizzical tone.

"Yeah," I said. I thought about telling him about the incident, but what good would it do. Of course, I might have sworn at the sailor in return, but that is exactly how people end up with a chipping hammer in their head in retaliation. He would have had no compunction about killing me if there were no one around. I suppose a tougher individual might have just invited him to the bottom of the tank to sort it out.

When he clambered out of the tank, ten minutes later, and saw that the bosun was there, he was all smiles and friendliness.

It took about thirty bucket lifts to clear each tank. I actually preferred being down the bottom, filling the buckets, to being at the top in the open air. This was because the mate would always put me on the other end of the radio with which he communicated from the cargo room. Each time I had hauled a bucket about thirty feet up, he would start trying to communicate with me on the radio. If I ignored him, he would just start screaming. Then, because it took so much longer to haul a full bucket up the remaining thirty feet than to drop it thirty feet back to the bottom, I would have to lower it, speak to him, and start all over again. I thought of pointing out to him that it would be more efficient to wait a little longer, but he could see what was going on from the little window in the cargo control room, so I worked out that he was simply making me suffer for making him look a fool over the gas-testing incident.

At one stage, the other cadet took over the radio while I was sent away to do something else and then was obliged to hang onto it for a while after I had come back. At the first opportunity, he got himself sent on an errand and handed it back to me with a satisfied little smile. I wasn't too bothered. I was a little bit older than him and I knew the truth of the, "The only person who'd never done anything wrong's never done anything," saying. It was better to take on a bit more and be shouted at occasionally than skive and never learn anything. When I became a captain, I was to find that loading the keener and better people down with work was unavoidable. It was pointless expending your energy on useless or lazy people because they weren't going to achieve anything. Sometimes, I would receive protests that I was being unfair, but I would simply say to the people onto whom I was piling the work, "Look at it this way, I think a lot of you, or I wouldn't be throwing all this in your direction."

I did hate having to look down the tanks while the others were hoovering or filling buckets. This wasn't just for the selfish reason that all the gas wafted up into my face; it was difficult to keep them in sight. I would shout down to see if they were all right. They couldn't make out what I was saying so they would move into the little circle of light cast through the butterworth hole I was looking through and shout up at me. When I said I was just checking if they were all right, I would be screamed at for dragging them away from their work. But what were you supposed to do. If you didn't hear from them for three minutes and they'd fallen over, gassed, and you didn't respond, they were brain damaged. Just to make the whole situation worse, you were expected to perform other tasks while you were supposed to be looking down the tanks, so you were continually being dragged away. I suppose I could just have taken the job more lightly, but the fact that they were happy not looking down all the time I was working at the bottom of the tanks wouldn't have justified my being happy not looking down all the time they were working at the bottom of the tanks.

You really had to be careful when the sailors were climbing up. It was important not to turn away just because they'd announced that they'd finished, and this wasn't just because they might fall off the ladder. The place a lot of those who did get gassed during tank-cleaning operations came to grief was the access hatch coaming, just as they were coming out because this is where some of the gas missed by the suction machines collected.

So, eventually, we were finished. The mate had done a good job: no one had died and no one was brain damaged or, at least, no one was acting any more brain damaged than before we started.

When you clean the tanks on board a tanker, you filter all the seawater which you've used to wash the tanks, before you pump it over the side. The oil residue which remains is pumped up to a tank on deck. Then you are supposed to pump it to a shoreside facility.

The mate had again done an excellent job, in terms of efficiency, and this tank was full with oil.

Something was going on. The mate had his narrow-eyed look which meant he was brooding on something, and the captain was rolling his eyes and biting his lip.

After a few days, the mate went out and pumped the contents of the oil tank straight over the side. What had gone on. Had the company been consulted. I don't think the ship would have done it without instructions from the company.

The environmental movement was just beginning to get fired up then. You wouldn't get away with this sort of thing nowadays. The authorities would want to check your receipts. They can work out how much residue you should have had on board over time and examine the figures signed for by the shore facilities to which you claimed to have discharged your settling tank.

I thought it was such a shame that the mate had done such a good job filtering all the residue out to only throw it over the side anyway. Some of this had been tricky, fiddling around checking separation levels etc. and it had all been a waste of time.

I'm convinced the company wouldn't have put anything in a telex; it would have all been done quietly on the satellite phone.

The company would definitely let the captain take responsibility if we were found out, not that the shore authorities would have gone after them.

The other cadet kept going on and on about this anti-environmental act. I wondered what he wanted to do. He didn't want to do anything, apart from going on and on complaining. I heard that on one of our other ships, with the same captain, the radio officer had moaned about a similar operation and let it be known that he'd taken photos. Subsequently, while he was working, someone went in his cabin and removed the film from his camera.

We still had a little while to go until we arrived at Singapore and the anti-American sailor collared me again, only this time he was steaming into the British Government. He started going on about leukaemia and the Greenham Common women. "What about them?" I said, only half-listening.

"It was all over the papers when we were in Australia last year," he said. "There are pictures of the Ministry of Defence police pointing radiation emitters at the women and they're coming down with leukaemia."

"Why isn't it in the British newspapers?" I said.

"Because it's D-Noticed," he replied. "The Australian newspapers asked the British editors why they didn't print the story and they said it was because it was D-Noticed." He had to explain what a D-Notice was. As I said, this was before the internet and when then were only two real conspiracy theories: over the assassination of President Kennedy and the Moon landings (or non-landings.)

"Still," he continued, "what can you expect of a Government which supports the Khmer Rouge?"

"Who are the Khmer Rouge?" I asked him.

"The ex-government of Cambodia," he said. "They killed two million people and our government supports them, or did."

'They wouldn't do that," I told him.

"You young boys are so naive," he said.

The mate, walking past, had caught a bit of this and he raised his eyes.

You found then that these men, so isolated, easily became monomaniacs. They also got involved in the study of some abstruse subjects even though you never saw them doing it. I sailed with a third mate once whom I'd never seen reading any books and whom it seemed never did anything, off-duty, apart from sit quietly in the officers' bar. Then, one night on the bridge, he suddenly turned to me and said, "Do you understand Einstein's laws of Special and General Relativity?" I replied that I most definitely did not. He then spent a patient hour explaining them and I swear that, at the time, I understood them. Since then, I've read four or five of those popular science books which attempt to explain them to the layman and I've never understood anything once they get beyond the man standing on the platform and the man sitting on the train and how they perceive the train to be moving at different speeds.

Singapore

The sailors were getting excited about Singapore. It was their joint favourite port with Santos in Brazil. They were excited about the women. I couldn't make out whether they hated or loved women. They would rant about women and I would think, yes, well I suppose you would hate women if the only women you ever met were whores demanding money from you and infecting you with venereal disease or wives kicking you out of your own home and moving their boyfriends in. And the next minute they would be threatening us cadets that, if they caught us being impolite to whores, they would knock our teeth out. They moaned about their wives, but if you murmured something sympathetic, they were capable of suddenly turning on you and giving you a ferocious verbal lashing for "slagging off" their beloveds.

One thing I was to notice in my time in the Merchant Navy was that the ones who claimed to be nasty to their wives were the ones who stayed married and the ones who went on and on about how marriage was the ideal lifestyle were the ones whose marriages failed. I sailed with one second mate on another company who spent as much of every leave as he could working short trips on coasters to support his family's lifestyle. His wife came onboard once and he was holding hands with her in the officers' mess and gazing at her so intently it was embarrassing. Then, later on, I found out that she had been having sex with the engineer cadet, whom she'd only just that minute met, in the second mate's own cabin while her husband was out on deck, working. She said she liked the danger of being found out. I suppose this opinion of womankind, which was forming in my mind though I was fighting it, as being willing to sleep with someone else and steal your home at the first opportunity and loving you more if you treat them badly is sexist but it's formed from listening to others' experiences for months on end.

During our approach to Singapore, the second mate took the cadets aside. "All is not what is seems in Singapore," he said, enigmatically. We were a little confused. We waited for him to explain further, but he didn't

The mate approached me out on deck. "I'm giving you both one day off," he said. We knew that this was only because the second mate had mentioned to the captain that the sailors were getting more time off than the cadets, which apparently wasn't the norm. There was some semblance of regulation about working hours for seamen who were sixteen or seventeen but there wasn't at that time any for those who were older so we just had to be grateful for any time off which we were given. "I'm going to try to give you the same day," the mate continued. I let out an involuntary groan. We cadets were not getting on. "Don't you want the same day off?" he said. "Eh, yeah, that'd be great," I replied. Cadets weren't supposed to have opinions or preferences and I knew that trying to apply conditions to an offer of a day off would be stupid.

We dropped anchor at Jurong and within minutes the boat was swarming with traders and prostitutes. I thought this was laughable. Imagine Fawley refinery just letting any third-world market trader or hooker, who wanted to, wander around their facilities. It'd be on the front page of every national newspaper the next morning, but, there we were, full of flammable liquid and heavy machinery, completely undefended. I haven't been deep-sea commercial since the new American-inspired security regulations came into force. I suppose it is all very different now.

I quietly asked the second mate why this was allowed. He said, "Well, look at it this way, a lot of people like the mate aren't going to have the opportunity to get off the ship and they want to buy something."

Western seamen were on their way out, however, and the traders had aimed their merchandise at third-world seamen on two dollars an hour and so most of it was rubbish. The mate, the tightest man I have ever met, bought his two fake Lacoste polos and fake Rolex, which were the only things he spent money on each trip. Some of the sailors bought some VHS porn cassettes.

I had a haircut in my cabin. It was the worst haircut I had ever had. I had picked the oldest and most ugly woman claiming to be able to cut hair on the basis that she probably wasn't a prostitute as I couldn't see her ever getting much custom if she were, and I didn't want someone piling on the pressure which the sailors said normally happened with the women claiming to be hairdressers. As soon as she finished, she said to me, "O.K. Now you want sex, thirty dollar?" "No," I told her. She held the point of her scissors to my jugular. "O.K., but you my customer, I find you went with other girl (despite being about fifty, she still thought of herself as a girl) I will kill you. O.K.?" I confirmed that I understood.

The mate enjoyed laughing and joking with the prostitutes, though he didn't have anything to do with them sexually. It was really weird. He never socialised normally, had no conversation, but enjoyed fraternising with them. The captain walked around with a frown. The chief engineer dispensed long opinions on the likelihood of catching HIV through various sexual acts. Almost every permutation appeared to have been considered.

There was a huge noise from the galley, and one fat prostitute was forcefully ejected. She had demanded food. The prostitutes had scissors; the cook had meat cleavers.

I considered this all another example of false advertising. I couldn't really say that the British Chamber of Shipping had given me any literature stating that the women with whom we could expect to consort were gorgeous hula girls in tropical ports, but certainly no one had made any attempt to disabuse me of this notion.

We went ashore in a launch the next morning. The captain had again been stingy with the advances. We were only on a pittance, but the captain still wouldn't advance much of it. "You'll need it when you're back at Warsash," he said. I suppose there was some logic in insisting that our funds ended up in the tills of the Great Harry and the Silver Fern rather than some Singaporean prostitute's purse.

The sailors were furious at having their advances restricted, though. The second mate insisted that the captain was doing the right thing. "Some of these guys will spend their entire wages and then go home with nothing for their two months leave if you let them," he said. The companies had all gone over to consolidated leave which meant that they just paid you a bit extra while you were on board and nothing when you were at home. It made life easier for them and they didn't have any of the captain's social concerns. They weren't that bothered about the sailors' welfare when they were on board; they certainly weren't bothered about what happened to them after they went home.

We climbed down into the launch, the sailors still grumbling that they were expected to enjoy a night out with a maximum of five hundred dollars. "I'm used to having a thousand dollars in my pocket in places like this," said one, bitterly.

The launch swiftly took us to Jurong pier and we were dumped by the sailors who had other things on their minds than looking after us.

Singapore reminded me of Crawley New Town, where I was from, only taller. I didn't really have any preconceptions. I had yet to read Somerset Maugham and ahis contemporaries and so I wasn't disappointed.

We went around the shops, but, as we didn't have much cash, that wasn't much fun. At five-thirty, we took the launch back to the tanker. The mate was surprised to see us. "What kind of cadets are you?" said the second mate. We were bemused. "What do you mean?" I asked. "Why didn't you go to the Red Lantern?" he said. "What's the Red Lantern?" we asked him. He shook his head, sadly.

The next day, we were all pumped up about the exotic entertainment available in Singapore, by the sailors. We were working all day but we were free to go ashore in the evening. The mate stomped up to us on deck. "So, you're thinking of going ashore tonight?" he said, aggressively. "Well, only because..." I started but he cut me off. "You know what time the boats back are?" he demanded. "Yeah, at midnight and at eight A.M," I answered him. He started jabbing me with his finger. "Don't think you're coming back on the eight A.M. boat," he said. "Your duty begins at eight A.M., and you won't get on board until ten-past on that launch, and it's 'yes chief', not 'yeah'." "But you only asked me what time the boats were and I told you," I said. "We don't have any intention of taking the morning launch." He jabbed me with his finger again, rocking me back. "No and you'd better not, Sonny," he said. Then he stomped off. "Cracked," said the other cadet. I thought so, too. The mate seemed normal but then, suddenly, he would go off on one. I found that was often the way in the Merchant Navy.

The second mate was going ashore, too. He was newly married and going around telling everyone how he wasn't having anything to do with any prostitutes, and all the sailors were going, "Yeah, yeah." I thought he was trying to reassure himself. Then, suddenly, the captain announced that he would be coming, too. I was interested in finding out what he was like off the boat. He was a tough guy. He'd been a street fighter in his native Yorkshire as a teenager and was notorious in the circles of his former tanker company for having beaten a massive sailor, a string of G.B.H. convictions guy, to a pulp with a steel torch when he'd been attacked at the manifold as a sixteen-year-old cadet. He'd done such a thorough job that the sailor hadn't been able to remember what had happened the next morning, unless of course, he was just trying to hide everything to save himself the embarrassment of having to admit he'd been beaten up by a kid.

Five-thirty rolled around and the sailors formed up at the top of the accommodation ladder. They were in the Merchant Navy going ashore uniform of fake Lacoste polo, shorts and trainers. Their hair was all clean and nicely combed and they actually looked happy for once. The cook ridiculed my attire, his Scouse accent making his observations sound funnier than they were. I thought I was dressed inoffensively in my white uniform shirt and jeans. The launch arrived and the sailors started looking impatient. They were waiting for the captain and the second mate. Eventually the pair of them appeared and we went down the ladder and into the boat and were whooshed into Jurong. The other cadet and I stood around onshore, and then some taxis appeared. The captain and the second mate got into one, and the sailors got into a pair of them. The cook shouted at us to join them, and we did, which was a big mistake. We should have tried to stay with the captain and the second mate.

First of all, we went to Newton Circus, a huddle of hawker stands. I don't know how the vendors managed to keep track of everything, but we just sat at a table and vendors from all the stands approached us and the sailors ordered bits and pieces from different ones. "What do you like?" The cook asked me. I shrugged. "Prawns?" I said. He smiled. "Prawns eh?" he said. "I'll get you prawns all right.

The vendors started piling up the food and eventually the table looked like one holding a slap-up meal out of the pages of the Beano. A plate was slid in front of me with a single, huge prawn which almost spilled over the side. "Like that?" said the cook. "Sure," I replied.

The food quickly disappeared. The sailors were ready to move onto their next venue. "What about the bills?" I said. "How much have you got?" said the cook. We showed him our pittances. He pushed our hands away. "We'll handle this," he said. They were quite generous. It was quite surprising. The sailors were all free and easy with their money and the officers were all tight gits.

Taxis took us to the strip and there were all these fat Americans and skinny Americans with perfectly trimmed moustaches, ranting at Asian girls in the street. "What's going on?" I asked the steward. "The American navy's in," he said. "The officers are the gay-looking ones." "Really?" I said.

"I've listened to you, now you listen to me," one fat American said to a girl at my side. She looked like she wanted to do some Thai kick-boxing thing on him. He turned to glare at me because I was listening, and I shrugged and followed the sailors into a bar. "They're not allowed in here," said the steward. "Isn't their money as good as ours?" I asked him. "Their shore patrol make it off-limits," he said. "Sometimes their shore patrol decide that other bars are off limits to anyone except their own boys." "How do they get away with that?" I asked him. "Ah, you can get in if you push it," he said, "but who wants the hassle. You'll only get into a fight and their shore patrol will take their own sailors' side."

I thought this bar was the final destination but it was just a warm-up and we were soon on our way to the Red Lantern.

I'd never been in any sort of nightclub. Crawley didn't have any and the whole clubbing culture hadn't yet taken off. "All these women are available," said the steward, bending down to whisper in my ear as we went inside.

Asian dolls were all over the place. The other male customers were the usual sixty and seventy-year-old, paunchy expatriates whom I found, over the years, infested such places, and a few American navy sailors, the more laid-back ones, not the, argumentative, fat slobs. On the way in, we passed a row of very angular-looking, tallish ladies dressed in heavily-sequined dresses. They smiled at me.

Soon, we were ensconced in banquettes while waitresses took our orders. I was quite surprised by how quickly a gang of tough Merchant Navy ratings assumed the pose of seventies lounge lizards.

A tide of prostitutes just seemed to sweep over us and I found myself engaged in conversation with a very smiley one who kept placing her hand on my knee but seemed to be looking at something past me. I turned to follow her gaze only to see the ladies' man steward looking nonchalantly at his drink, his long blonde hair flopping over his eyes. The captain had told us that Singaporean girls loved long hair on men as the place was still a little repressed. In the early seventies, he'd said, the only men who could get into the country with long hair were sailors because the state had such a hatred of hippies that any arriving at the airport were forced to have a haircut before they were allowed through immigration.

I was soon struggling with the level of alcohol consumption which was expected and the consequent full bladder. I got up and went to find the toilets.

Just as I was at a urinal, one of the angular-looking ladies came up to the adjoining facility and it was quite clear that she was actually a man. She smiled at me, benignly. The second mate's enigmatic statement about all not being what it seemed in Singapore suddenly became clear. The ladyboy phenomenon had yet to enter the public consciousness and my only exposure to the idea of transvestites or transsexuals had been through the occasional TV appearance of Dame Edna Everidge.

I went over to our table. "Those ladies are men," I said.

"KaiThais," said the vicious sailor who, unfortunately, had accompanied us. He was busily groping his woman who, it turned out, was his regular squeeze in Singapore.

Suddenly, I realised that the steward had his arm around my girl. He was looking at me idly as if wondering what I was going to do. The bosun was also looking at me. What was I supposed to do. Was I supposed to challenge him. It was quite feasible that these men would fight over prostitutes. There weren't any other women such as wives and girlfriends around to fight over. I wondered what would happen if I said anything. Would he just say, "Take her back." Were they just playing with me. Did they even bring me and the other cadet along with them just to pick fights with us. Suddenly, the girl said, "You don't mind?" "Eh, no," I replied. Everyone stopped looking at me.

It's never a good idea to get into a fight with merchant seamen. They don't normally have the option of running away in their minds as they are used to being stuck with their prospective opponent on a ship, so can be quite ferocious and, of course, they all carry knives. Plus, they practically have to kill their opponent before they can expect any sanction as the authorities and the companies don't really care what happens to them. Legal authority at sea is one huge grey area which a lot of sex criminals are finding, to their delight, on cruise ships.

Another prostitute suddenly spotted a vacancy and smiled at me from across the room and then sat down next to me. She had short boyish hair and I wondered briefly if she were a ladyboy. I whispered my suspicions to the steward. "Ask her," he said, "she won't mind you asking."

"Are you a KhaiThai?" I asked, politely.

"I girly girl," she said, without seeming to be in the slightest offended. If I'd had more experience, I would have known. The ladyboys were not going to have boyish haircuts. For them, it was long silky hair, anything to emphasise their femininity.

"Dance with her," said the steward.

We hit the floor and she asked me if I wanted to go to a hotel with her for sixty dollars.

"I don't have that much money," I said.

She smiled sweetly. "I would like to marry someone like you and live here forever," I continued. She smiled even more sweetly. Then I saw her looking in the direction of an American sailor who was casting admiring glances at her.

"I'm sorry," she said and she drifted over to him.

Sadly, I went and sat down again.

"What happened?" Said the steward.

"She went over to that American," I replied.

"Probably offended that you asked her if she were a KhaiThai," he mused.

Bloody hell, I thought. I was about to protest that only a moment before he'd advised me to do just that but there was too much going on, and he wouldn't have listened anyway.

Some of the sailors disappeared with various members of Singapore's sex industry workforce and the remainder of us piled into taxis, but only after we'd all tried to get into rickshaws. The drivers had balked at the overloading on which the sailors had tried to insist.

Soon, we were waiting for the launch. I suddenly realised that there were a couple of hookers with us. Were they being brought back to the ship? They certainly were.

Hard to imagine now, but this was par for the course then.

It was exciting, speeding through the anchorage at night, between the other ships, and then clambering onto the accommodation ladder.

The sailors and the girls disappeared, and we went up to our cabins on the officers' deck.

The next morning, I came out of my cabin and walked along to the top of the staircase in front of the captain's cabin. Just then, one of the prostitutes appeared, seemingly from out of nowhere. She looked as though she were lost. I was just about to ask her what she wanted and then the captain came out of his cabin, accompanied by the superintendent, who'd arrived the previous evening. "I'll see you later, Sunshine. Now get her out of here," he said.

Alarmed, I tugged at the prostitute's sleeve and dragged her down to the galley. "Ah, there you are," said the cook to her. "Terry's been looking for you."

I went into the control room and then the mate's phone rang, and he sent me upstairs to the captain's cabin.

He sat behind his desk, fuming. "I am responsible for old whores you bring on board," he said, red-faced. I thought the old whore bit was a little unchivalrous but listened patiently. This was difficult. I didn't know what was going on here. It was quite stupid really. He'd let all the hookers from the bum boats on board but was furious about the couple that had been brought back last night. That didn't seem rational. Plus, he clearly thought she was with me, but, if I said anything, even though the sailors didn't seem to be held to the same standard and probably wouldn't be fined or anything, they would think of it as splitting. Best just to keep silent and take the abuse. He ranted on for a while longer and then kicked me out.

The mate was smiling when I got into the

control room again. He obviously found this whole prostitute business highly amusing. "So, you discharged dirty ballast, did you?" he asked. I just looked remorseful. I didn't want to say yes and then be found out to have been lying and I didn't want to say no and then be accused of splitting.

Later on, I saw the second mate, normally the voice of reason, on the bridge. He knew the truth. "I don't understand why he was so tolerant of the random prostitutes on the bum boats but is so furious about this one," I said.

"You were so blatant," he said, "marching her straight past his cabin.

"But she wasn't with me," I said.

"Irrelevant," he replied. "It looked like she was."

"He'll find out from someone," I said.

"He will; someone will delight in telling him," he said, "and then you'll really be in it because you'll have caused him embarrassment by omission of a clarification for which he knows full well you would have risked a chipping hammer to the head or at least a smack in the face."

"It's not fair," I said.

"Welcome to the Merchant Navy," he told me. "You could have got a job in an office. The only professions which society and the Government respect are the legal profession and accountancy," he repeated. "You made the decision to join a dying industry and now you're flapping about with it in its death throes." He was quite a poet when he wanted to be. "Ah, just forget it," he said. "Half those A.B.s will have a dose now and the captain will have something else to fume about. He'll have to issue the antibiotics to them, and they'll be supposed not to drink while they're taking them and they'll drink anyway, and the diseases won't go away, and it'll go on and on. I just hope they haven't picked up Vietnamese Rose."

"What's that?" I said.

"Horrible, really nasty disease the Vietnamese prostitutes used to try to infect the G.I.s with. Makes your member look like a rose."

"Or HIV," I said."

"HIV, there are no symptoms," he replied. "Not until you start to die anyway." On that cheerful note, I left him to his charts.

The next morning, the other cadet approached me, walking slowly along the deck, evidence of his hangover in his unsteady progress. We weren't getting on at all now, and I dreaded every moment with him. The surveyors were coming today to look at the tanks before we loaded for a return trip to Yokohama. I wondered what he wanted.

"The mate asked me if all the tanks were dry," he said.

"So?" I replied.

"I told him I might remember a puddle," he said.

"You did what?" I asked him. He just looked at me. "Which one?" I said. I had a hammering hangover myself.

"I don't know," he replied.

"So?" I said.

"So, the mate said we have to check every single one," he announced. What! I couldn't believe it.

"Unbelievable," I said. "You are just a

disaster."

"Well, I'll do them all," he pleaded.

"Oh yeah," I said. "That'll look great won't it, my standing around at the top of all the tanks while you go down." He just looked sulky. His lantern jaw and the few wisps which he was trying to pretend was a moustache offended me even more than usual. I just said. "Let's get on with it."

We had to go up and down the sixty-foot ladders in twenty-one tanks and walk around, tripping over stringers, our heads spinning. The mate knew the state we were in. He was taking a risk really. If one of us had fallen off a ladder or tripped over a stringer and smashed our head and died, questions would have been asked. He was the tightest git in the Merchant Navy but all those pennies he'd scrupulously saved over the years would have soon gone on grasping lawyers.

It was quite surprising the treatment cadets got. One well-known oil company sent a newly arrived first trip, sixteen-year-old engineer cadet straight down the engine room for a whole day in the Gulf, in temperatures well over forty degrees centigrade. When he came up, he went up to his cabin and died. The company faked a little bit of sympathy and issued a few guidelines. My mate was on another of that company's ships when they were circulated, and the chief engineer had walked into the officer's bar, slapped them down, and said, "If you follow these, I'll fire you." The companies can always get new sixteen-year-olds if they kill some.

There was none of this rescue team business now. The tanks were regarded as completely safe; they'd been cleaned so long ago. We didn't even bother watching each other; we just went down a different tank each at the same time. The mate would be spying on us from his window. Any slacking or missing out of tanks and we would be subject to his finger jabbing and ranting again.

I felt terrible. I thought I was going to faint. I was a little bit worried about being shut in as well. That was a bigger risk than suffocating at that point. Later on, I shut a hatch on a man down a tank while we were tank-cleaning, but, luckily, the youngest and nicest sailor had happened to be walking past just as I finished doing it and mentioned that there was someone down this tank, and I had been able to open the hatch before anyone noticed, and he didn't tell anyone.

Once we'd finished, I suddenly thought that we'd been very stupid. We should have told the mate that we found this mysterious puddle in the first tank we went down. We never actually found any puddles, so it wouldn't have made any difference.

We went into the control room and slumped onto the couch and told him that all the tanks were dry. He smiled his little smile. He knew they were. He'd been punishing us for wanting to go ashore instead of being dedicated and staying on the boat. He'd never gone ashore when he was a cadet but I'm sure it wasn't due to professionalism but to his being a tight Northern git.

That night, something very strange happened to me. I suddenly found myself standing in darkness in complete panic. I was convinced I was shut in a tank. I started screaming and hammering on the bulkheads, but no one came. I started clawing at the bulkhead and then thrashing around. Suddenly, my hand hit something and I realised it was a phone. What was a telephone doing inside a tank, I asked myself. Then I understood. I wasn't inside a tank; I was in my cabin. I clawed my way along the wall and found the light switch and turned the light on. I wasn't asleep. I was fully awake. I had never sleep-walked, so I hadn't been sleeping. I had been awake and genuinely thought I was trapped inside a tank. Even weirder, I had exactly the same experience the next night. I wondered if I were going insane. Were all those, dangerous, carcinogenic chemicals we were breathing in as part of our professional apprenticeship affecting my brain. I didn't know. I didn't want to say anything, either. If they thought I genuinely was going round the twist, they might fire me.

If you went missing, it wasn't certain that they'd come looking for you straight away or even at all. With limited crews, no one wants to search through twenty-one cargo tanks or the hundreds of other spaces, looking for you, especially someone unimportant like a cadet. It's easier just to write in the log "missing," and leave it as assumed that you fell over the side. If they find you later on, dead somewhere, oh well, life will go on, for everyone else.

I went back to sleep. I was completely drenched in sweat. I'd been more frightened than I'd ever been in my life.

There were stories of welders being trapped inside compartments during builds. One container ship belonging to a well-known

British line had always been considered an unlucky vessel. After a few years of sailing, it went into a shipyard for some work, and, during the yard period, the shipyard cut into a compartment and found a welder who'd gone missing during the build.

The steward went home, complete with horrible dose and a bottle of antibiotics. Shouldn't have stolen that girl from me, eh, I thought.

There was a new steward on board, a young tough from Birmingham, who spent his time, in between moaning fits, working out with weights in the room which passed for a gym, the weights being the only facilities. The only other option for passing the time was this mousetrap game in which you spent forever building this complicated trap and tried to catch a plastic mouse. There were supposed to be three mice but, in typical company style, there were only two. Someone's child had left it behind years ago.

I soon had a run-in with the new steward. I made some flippant remark, and he took offence and started throttling me while I was having lunch. The only other person in the room was the engineer cadet, who was facing me. I could feel myself fainting and knocked the steward's arm aside. the engineer cadet looked terrified. I was gasping and wheezing too much to be frightened. Suddenly, the steward smashed me in the face. I got up and looked at him. He wore a smug, self-satisfied smile. The cook had entered the messroom and was standing with arms folded, looking on with pride while his boy knocked about a junior officer. I wondered what to do and then I suddenly thought, better to go down fighting, and hit him as hard as I could in the face. To my amazement, he just gawped at me in astonishment. Then the engineer cadet got in between us and tried to hold us apart. I thought I had better do as much damage as I could to the steward while he was still surprised and threw myself over the top of the engineer cadet to get at him, but, just then, the cook piled in, threw his arms around the steward, and said, "That's enough." He'd been quite happy to stand around, looking on when his boy was getting the best of it, but he'd had a sudden change of heart once I had retaliated and he thought I might win. He bundled him off out of the mess room.

"You'll be in trouble now, Willy," said the engineer cadet.

"He started it," I protested.

"You started it by striking at his arm," he said.

"He was throttling me at the time," I insisted. "You're a witness."

"You both are to blame," he said. "I have to be fair." Bloody hell. He was supposed to be my mate. We'd been together on this boat for months, and he was Irish. I thought the Irish always backed up their mates. I pointed this out to him. He shook his head ruefully. "I have to be fair," he said.

I went up to the bridge. I was on watch with the second mate. He looked at me, strangely. "You're bleeding," he said.

"Oh, I banged my head on a door," I replied. If the captain found out about this little fight, he'd probably have to send both of us home to cover himself. If it were sailors, he could be reasonably confident he'd never hear anything from the company, but with boys involved, you never knew. The second mate looked dubious.

One of the sailors came up, one of the ones who normally treated us cadets with contempt. He smiled at me for the first time. "All right, Willy?" he said. He seemed to be looking at me with some admiration. If only I'd known it was that simple. Probably Warsash should have advised us, "When you get on board, just find someone bigger and harder than yourself and hit him as hard as you can and you'll get along a lot better than you will otherwise."

The second mate had had his lunch on the bridge.

"Here, take that down to the galley," he said, passing me his plate.

I took it down and found the steward looking at me. Was he going to have another go. "You didn't say anything, did you?" he asked.

"I just said I banged my head on a door," I said. I wiped my face and looked at my hand. It was covered in blood.

"It'll stop bleeding soon," said the steward. I looked at him. I was disappointed that I hadn't cut him or at least given him a black eye.

He was as nice as pie to me after that, and I stopped throwing flippant remarks in his direction. I never really trusted the engineer cadet again, though.

This was the only violence I experienced on this trip but you can see how unjustified it is of Warsash to throw boys out for fighting when they know full well the sort of environment into which they are going to be sending them. Much better to give them training in fighting rather than lectures on their responsibility to uphold the law and all that other stuff which they seem to have got out of C.S. Hornblower.

One evening, we cadets were alone in the bar with the captain. He was feeling quite relaxed and we ended up sat down at the table, listening to him. He started out happily enough, but then he became slightly morose. He'd spent all his time on tankers and quite a lot of that on chemical tankers. These are the ships which carry the most-evil cargoes. They are highly dangerous.

I mentioned some whispers I'd heard at college about them: people running up the decks with their faces burning off, their eyes gone. "All true," he said. "I've seen it. But," he continued, "you always get a night in port because they're only allowed to leave in daylight." Great, I thought. At the price of being blinded, burnt or killed!

There were some easy ways to do this to yourself, according to him. With some cargoes, you had to wear breathing apparatus beneath sealed suits. Some people would just undo their zip slightly to let all their exhaled breath out of the suit while standing at the manifold rather than walking all the way back to the cargo room. This was fine if the manifold weren't leaking, but if it were, then the cargo vapour would get straight inside the suit. "I remember one boy," he started to say. Then he thought better of giving us all the gory details. "Well, the bosun managed to rinse his eyes and save his sight," he quickly concluded.

Seamen age quickly anyway but I met some chemical tanker men later on and their faces were the faces of old men so I didn't believe all the 'It's fine if you follow the safe working practices', gumpf.

I saw the mate looking in at us through the bar door. I knew he wouldn't like this, our having a little tete a tete with the Capitano. We might pay for it later on.

The captain continued. "That naptha we're taking up to Yokohama is carcinogenic," he said. Great, I thought again. Sooner or later, we would have to get down inside the tanks and breathe in all the fumes while we moped up the remains.

Then the new chief engineer came in. The captain and he smiled and were friendly, but we'd heard that there was a long-time enmity between these two. Sure enough, after a few minutes of pleasantries, it started. "Why don't you like me?" demanded the chief.

"I just don't know, if I'm honest," said the captain. The chief was quiet for a moment and then he started up again. It was a little bit embarrassing. Normally when things like this began, we were thrown out of the bar but the captain and the chief engineer were secure enough not to worry about what a couple of cadets thought about them. We wanted to leave but couldn't think of a polite way to extricate ourselves. I almost wished the mate would come in with a job for us. If we hadn't wanted him to, we could have been sure he would have.

Finally, I just edged my chair back and said that I had to do some studying. The other cadet followed my lead. The captain and the chief didn't even seem to notice, and we both quietly slipped out.

As I went past the mate's cabin, he called out sarcastically, "Enjoying a little soirée with the captain, were you?". I turned round, trying to think of some reason for having been socialising beyond my pay grade, but couldn't. He would fume now.

Return to Yokohama

Having loaded, we set sail for the return trip to Yokohama. The weather was fine and everyone was satiated after their illicit adventures in Singapore, and, on the first Sunday afternoon, the mate reluctantly acceded to the request that the pool was filled and we lounged around in our Speedos. Soon, people were doing somersaults off the deck above. Someone was going to hurt himself very badly, I thought. I'm sure that in today's health and safety climate, such antics would not be permitted.

No one wanted to fight. All the seething resentments and the brooding on slights long forgotten by those who'd delivered them had come to the fore in drink-filled exchanges in the likes of The Red Lantern and now everyone was matey. Even I and the steward were on friendly terms.

Having been sent down to fetch more beers though, I was accosted by the strange figure of the bosun. "You see the officer's wives up there sometimes, flaunting themselves in their bikinis. You know what rape is then," he said, quietly. We didn't have any wives on board which, having listened to the stories of Mrs Captain and Mrs Chief indulging themselves in casual use of their arbitrary authority and of the junior wives causing mayhem by sleeping with the more handsome and muscular sailors was, I thought, probably a godsend. I just murmured something and walked on.

I took the beers up and strolled onto the bridge deck and round to the wings. The second officer was there, slumped over the bulwark, nursing a hangover. "How's the party?" he asked.

"All right," I said. "Capitano's not there, and the mate keeps looking on, grumpily.

"He's a machine," said the second mate off-handedly, "only way to survive." He didn't seem to be much of a machine himself and he was surviving, though he did look thirty-five and was only twenty-five. "I can't believe I slept with a whore in Singapore," he said. "I'm happily married."

"I bet your cabin's clean," I said slyly. He gave me a querulous look. I'd noticed that whenever the sailors slept with some really dirty prostitute, they always scrubbed their cabin the next day, some psychological thing no doubt.

"You didn't do anything," he said, "after going on about it." I'd never mentioned the possibility of sleeping with any prostitutes. He was imagining it.

"Not my fault if the captain won't advance us any money," I said. "He's your buddy."

"He's not my buddy," said the second mate. "I am his protégé." You could get away with talking like that to the second mate. The third mate would have been all offended. The mate would have slammed you into a bulkhead.

To Jeddah

Two more sailors joined in Yokohama and a gang of Thais who were going to do nothing except chip and paint for five or six months.

One of the sailors was a Liverpudlian. He had white-blonde hair and was in his thirties and I'm sure women would have loved him but his face was mottled with thin veins due to drink. He had that Liverpudlian talent for always seeming funny whatever he was saying. A joke that would not have raised a smile if told by someone else seemed hilarious when told by him. The ship needed someone happy on board. It was good to have him around.

There was a revelation once we'd left Yokohama, got rid of the carcinogenic naptha, and were on our way to Jeddah and were cleaning the tanks. For some reason, they'd decided to send two of us down a tank at the same time and I was hoovering and mopping away in the pools of water and I heard this amazing singing. I looked round and there was the Liverpudlian standing in a pool of light which passed through one of the Butterworth holes, singing at the top of his voice, and the acoustic effect produced by the tank made it sound like he was singing at the Royal Albert Hall. He looked at me and smiled and then went back to work. "What are you doing here?" I asked him. "You should be on the stage." I thought he'd have been great in a pier theatre or in Blackpool, in a dinner jacket, telling a few jokes to the old grannies, and then bursting into song. He just needed a manager. If I'd had any business ability at all, I would have been straight over to him with a proposition and a contract.

"Don't know," he said. "I was working on the sites and then I got onto a dredger and then I eventually managed to get into the seamen's union and now I'm here."

"You've got talent," I said. "It's such a waste."

"Life's for living, not for dreaming," he said.

I liked him a lot. A few nights later, when the drink was flowing and I'd made some flippant remark (I had to stop doing that) some of the other sailors manipulated events until the Liverpudlian and I were facing each other on the poop deck.

"Willy," he said, "do you really want to hurt me?"

"Of course not," I said. "I like you. Who says I'd win anyway?" Then he smiled and walked back inside and I followed him, much to the disappointment of the manipulators who'd so wanted to see a fight.

He was not so popular with the officers, who were generally Geordies or Yorkshiremen apart from the third mate. They didn't seem to like Scousers on principle. Being from the South, my only exposure to them had been to comedians on the television, so I just thought of them all as entertainers.

The other new sailor was a boy from Colchester. He spent every single moment of his leaves backpacking, mostly in South East Asia and therefore got on well with the Thais and even spoke a little bit of their language. With his Roman nose, angular face and thin black moustache, he even resembled them slightly and I was once sent looking for him and stood asking at the door of the Thais' mess room as to whether they'd seen him, without realising that he was sitting in the middle of their little gang.

He was only twenty-two and thus more on our wavelength than the older, slightly more-bitter sailors and the much more-bitter officers. He still enjoyed life in the Merchant Navy. He also didn't get bogged down in the political machinations and the ever-shifting feuds which dominated life on board.

It was strange: the ship was still the same ship, but the change of a few personnel made it seem like a different one. Of course, a change of captain was what really made a difference, but I'd only sailed with one captain so far so I didn't know that yet. I was later to have my best and worst times at sea on one ship during a single trip during which we had a change of captain halfway through. A paranoid, bitter, highly aggressive, Northern Irish captain was replaced by a laid-back, British public-school type and, overnight, the oppressive atmosphere lifted.

We'd got rid of the vicious sailor with the string of G.B.H. convictions. He'd gone home with an horrific dose. I was disappointed that he'd never been beaten up by the bosun, but he was always careful to only pick on us boys or other sailors who were smaller and more passive than he.

The bosun had also changed. We'd heard things about the new bosun before he arrived in

Yokohama. Apparently, he always travelled with his wife and the second engineer said that when he'd sailed with him on a previous occasion, he'd been uncertain exactly who was the bosun, him or his Mrs.

He strolled up the gangway, his wife bringing up the rear, and smiled. This was something the previous bosun had never done. His wife surveyed the scene. She seemed to be looking the mooring arrangements over.

This bosun was quite old and some of the sailors were a bit suspicious of him. It was known that he had a discharge book number which began with UK instead of an R which meant it had been issued not so many years ago when he would have been in his thirties, and it was thought that he was ex-Royal Navy which was anathema to the Merchant Navy guys. They hadn't forgotten the insult when, despite losing more members than any other service, they, along with the wounded, weren't allowed to take part in the victory parade after the war because Churchill thought they would make it look scruffy.

I liked the new bosun. He just spoke normally to me and there wasn't the constant threat of a punch in the face which there had been with the previous one. Whether that meant he couldn't control the crew or not, I didn't yet know. According to the ranks of management books in the bookshops at home, you didn't need the threat of violence to instill discipline in a workforce but, so far, from what I'd seen, at sea, you did.

He'd no sooner dumped his bags in the cabin and come out on deck in a bright orange boiler suit than he got into an argument with the mate. One of the things which the tiresome shore authorities in their ignorance bang on and on about is the gangway net. It is supposed to catch you if you fall off the gangway. It wouldn't, but never mind. It's typical of the distortion of priorities caused by the lack of experience of the people who draft the regulations that the authorities don't mind you being gassed and exposed to carcinogens down a cargo tank but they don't want you walking up a perfectly safe gangway without a net. The mate told the bosun to rig up the gangway net. He said that it was a Japanese gangway and they should rig the net up. The mate asked him if he wanted to put our own gangway out. The bosun said something back, and the mate invited him round to the poop deck. I thought the mate would kill him, but they both emerged unscathed. Later on, I heard the mate saying to the captain that he wanted the new bosun off. The captain murmured something.

I asked the second mate, always the voice of reason, when sober at least, what he thought of all this. "He's just come on and he's started agitating," he said, "Fire him."

The bosun wasn't fired. The company probably didn't want to pay another airfare.

The deck immediately spilt up. I, the bosun and the Liverpudlian were on one side; the other cadet and most of the other A.B.s were on the other, with the young A.B. neutral. I had tried to remain neutral, but I was too friendly to the new bosun and so considered to be in his camp.

The bosun probably saved my life. One of the deckhands was a miserable, old Scot and had come from submarines, although that didn't seem to encourage him to align with the bosun, and we were going to paint the accommodation and I asked him to tie the knot in my safety rope. "Tie your own bloody knot," he said. I considered this, but spoke to the bosun. He tied it for me. "You should learn how to tie your own knot, Willy," he said. "I might have been on the wacky-backy, you don't know. You shouldn't trust someone else. Did you explain to him that you didn't know how to tie the knot?" "I did," I said. "He said he didn't care." "Well, to be honest," said the bosun, "I don't think he knows how to tie the knot." This was probably true. We were going out on the planks, sitting on them, high above the deck, the only thing holding the plank up being the friction of the three turns of rope that you wrapped round it. This sailor just refused to do this job. He said he was scared of heights and he got away with it. The other sailors were furious. "He gets paid the same," they said, "and we're fed up with him saying he doesn't know how to do things. It's always like that. He doesn't have to splice multi-plat (a difficult job). He just says he doesn't know how to and that's that."

Anyway, I went out on the plank with the young sailor. We were half way down the accommodation, and I was feeding the loops of rope around the plank, which was how you lowered yourself, and the whole rope suddenly flicked off. The plank fell vertical, held up only at the sailor's end and I was dangling on the end of the safety rope. Had the bosun just insisted, as had the ex-submariner, that I tied it myself and I'd got it wrong, I might have been a goner. Having originally just wound up in the bosun's camp by default, I was now an enthusiastic member.

We got to Singapore again and took bunkers. I made it up the road, this time with the steward. I wasn't a big fan of his, but he had decided that, since our little fracas, we were good mates, and I preferred his company to that of the other cadet anyway. It wasn't easy to avoid going ashore with people with whom you didn't want to. There seemed to be some unspoken rule that anyone could join any party. It was strange, too, that age didn't seem to matter. You might find a twenty year old, a forty year old and a sixty year old all going for a night out together and the varied ages never really affected anything. Whether it had been like that before minimum manning came in, I didn't know.

We went to an area where the girls all stood in little lines in front of by-the-hour hotels. They were formed like a military unit awaiting inspection, dainty little handbags in place of Lee Enfield's. The steward immediately disappeared with a girl and then reappeared ten minutes later with a big smile on his face, and we sat outside of a corner bar, drinking Tiger beer and observing the comings and goings.

There was no evidence of our fight. The cut on my face had healed up and his face had never been marked anyway. I had been lucky. Surprise had counted for everything.

We actually started to get on. He didn't start griping about everyone else on the ship which would have been standard Merchant Navy procedure. Moaning was an easy trap to fall into. You could go down the other routes, like the mate who'd just turned himself into a machine, or like some of the engineers who couldn't talk about anything apart from the main engine, but most just drifted into constant moaning.

The steward called one girl over who was strangely dressed in camouflage and started trying to negotiate a deal for both of us to go with her at the same time. Luckily, negotiations fell flat. He was too cheap.

I wondered what it was like here in the old days of Bugis Street when the British Merchant Navy was at its height. I kept hearing about this world, which had collapsed. It was quite depressing to have missed out. The Merchant Navy had been a way of life and now they were trying to make it just a job.

'Cut costs, cut costs, cut costs.' That was the mantra of all these shore managers who drove company Audis and sent themselves off on courses on the latest IMO, waste of time, conventions.

"Come on, Willy, let's go back," said the steward after a while.

We went back to Jurong to wait on the launch.

I missed a launch in La Spezia, later on, still a cadet, on another of the company's ships. It wasn't entirely my fault; I was run over. I woke up in hospital and the hospital tried to throw me out, but, having no idea where the hospital was, and being covered in road grit and blood, I wouldn't leave the premises.

The captain - a different captain - finally came and found me after he'd had a nice lunch, accused me of wasting the company's money (the hospital hadn't given me any attention, so I couldn't see there being much of a bill) and told me to follow my nose and walk back to the jetty (we were still in the same town). I pointed out that I was covered in road grit and blood and didn't have any money and it was about ninety degrees, and he just said, "That's your own fault."

It took me two hours, staggering around, asking directions from frightened Italians, to find the jetty and, just as I arrived, the captain turned up in a taxi, got out, gave me a filthy look and sauntered into an ice cream parlour and ordered himself a massive ice cream.

I went and stood next to him. "What do you want?" he said.

"I'm thirsty, Captain," I told him. He reluctantly pulled out about a pound's worth of Lira.

"I'll sub you this until we get back to the boat," he said.

I had a friend who gave up the sea to become a marine lawyer. He succeeded wildly at this profession and ended up with a beach house in Brazil and all the other trappings of wealth.

"But how can you do this profession in which you're helping to sling into jail poor captains who've simply been trying to do their job?" I asked him.

"Think of all those captains who treated you badly over the years," he replied, "wouldn't you be happy to see them slung in jail?" and I thought of this particular captain.

Once we'd left Singapore, bound for Jeddah, I was sent down the engine room for engine room experience. We weren't going to be ever working in the engine-room, although, thanks to the utterly stupid system, we were expected to perform engineering on some of the deck equipment from day one without any experience or any engineering training. Again, imagine that in a refinery on shore. There is now way that the authorities or the companies would let completely untrained people start attempting to maintain the pipelines and valves, but the Merchant Navy was out of sight and out of mind.

It got me away from the other cadet as the second engineer said he only wanted one of us down there at a time.

I thought he was going to give me the dirtiest, most dangerous jobs, but the engineers weren't really motivated to persecute us. They were just happy to have different company for a week.

The engine-room itself was a hellhole: it was noisy, it stunk even worse of diesel than the rest of the ship, the vibration was horrible, there was high voltage electricity everywhere.

The engineers all had terrible skin owing to the environment in which they worked and some of the older ones had difficulty in hearing.

They liked to call themselves engineers but most of them were mechanics, really. I was laid into by someone once over this distinction, a captain strangely. He said something about another captain who'd insisted that the engineers weren't proper engineers. I offhandedly said, "Well, I think there's something about you having to be a chartered engineer to call yourself an engineer in the Government's eyes." The captain became very angry. I should have just kept my mouth shut.

The engineers' refuge was the control room, an air-conditioned sanctuary. I naively thought that the air-conditioning was for their benefit, but when the second engineer found out that I harboured this illusion, he laughed and told me it was to protect the electronics.

They were more relaxed than the deck officers but then they weren't really legally responsible for anything. The deck officers spent their entire lives risking jail for some professional mistake. Engineers who made mistakes just got fired, rang up an agency, and got on board another boat.

They gave me a few jobs to do, nothing technical. They were just happy nattering.

On a previous ship, the second engineer, against his better judgement, had given a deck cadet a more involved task, and the deck cadet had made such a disaster of it that the second had drawn a circle in chalk on the bottom plates and told the cadet that, other than for meals or to go to the toilet, he wasn't to move out of that circle for his entire engine-room time.

The engineers were at peace at the moment. Since the new chief engineer had come, there hadn't been any political troubles. The new chief engineer had no personality, so there had been little possibility of a personality clash with any of his staff.

The only time he sounded vaguely

human was when he bemoaned his father's insistence that he become an engineer instead of a baker. He seemed to spend most of his life dreaming of this other life as a baker on which he was missing out. It might be easier to understand if he'd dreamed of being a professional footballer or an actor or something, and been thwarted, but to mourn the fact that you'd missed out on a career as a baker seemed unusual, although I suppose every profession has equal validity. Who is to judge one as being more worthy of desire than another.

I was in a little world of dreamers. Almost all of the men on board mourned the loss of their one "True love:" the girl from school they should have married, the stripper who'd seemed to genuinely like them and whom they should have invited out for a drink which they believed would have inevitably led to a life of blissful cohabitation.

I'd see, in my time, tough captain after tough captain grasping his drink and cursing himself for not marrying some girl or other and never thinking to spend some of that energy he was wasting trying to improve relations with the woman he had actually married.

We made our way up the Malacca Straits. This was during the height of the piracy problem. People laugh if you tell them that there is modern day piracy but it exists and it's a pretty vicious business. Whole ships have been stolen, the crew never having been seen again. One of my friends sailed with some people who'd been on a ship which was attacked. The pirates had demanded the combination to the safe from the captain, and the captain being British and having seen too many Jack Hawkins films, had adopted a stiff upper lip and refused to give it up. They ripped opened his scrotum. He wouldn't tell. They pulled all his tubes out. He wouldn't tell. They were just about to wield the knife and the chief officer, who also had the combination, gave it up. People get carried away. They don't realise the company doesn't care and the money's insured and it isn't as if the insurance company was going to pay that money out to the widows and orphans who hold their policies. It was just going to steal it and pay its shareholders fat dividends.

The British Government is far more concerned that you don't cause an international incident and involve them by killing or injuring any pirates. They issue fatuous advice about dousing the pirates with fire hoses. That's just what you want isn't it, a soaking wet, extremely angry pirate. As if he's going to say, "I won't use my Kalashnikov because they might douse me with their firehouse again." The advice from the Government actually warns against getting them involved. The pirates have human rights; seamen don't.

I was once, when I was younger and more inclined to advocate fighting back, subjected to a lecture from a young Miss, a Guardian reader and sociology student, on how pirates are underprivileged and we shouldn't resent them. I could have mentioned their tendency to gangbang ship's wives. What would she want us to do about that: respect the pirates' underprivileged status or the women's right not to be violated?

There are some amusing stories though. I heard about one captain who was kidnapped by Nigerian pirates. He didn't actually have that bad a time while in captivity: the chief kept him well fed and constantly supplied with female company. However; he was surprised to find that, upon his release, the company told him it considered his time in captivity to be an unapproved absence from the vessel and it was therefore counting it as part of his annual leave.

The Government always pays lip service to protecting merchant seamen. It was the same with the tanker war in the Gulf. The Government made a big deal of the Royal Navy's Armadillo patrol. However, as soon as the ships got to the really dangerous bit, the Armadillo patrol turned round and headed for home.

Our ship had some steel just in front of the bridge doors. This had been our company's only consideration to safety from missiles during the tanker war.

The sailors who did sail on the ships during that conflict got war pay but only for the actual days they were in the war zone, so they got double pay for three or four days. Big deal. And the companies used the same old, 'You fight for your comrades', Army psychology to get them to go. Technically, the sailors could demand to be put off the vessel before it entered the war zone but very few did. They didn't want to be seen to be letting the rest of the crew down. Yet, who would they really have been letting down, a gang of vicious, ruthless crooks, sitting in nice oil company offices in Britain or the States.

We rigged up some fire hoses and mounted more deck watches. The captain actually seemed a bit nervous, which was unusual.

The sailors said that by far the best anti-piracy measure was to paint Haifa on the stern. The pirates don't mess with Israelis and if the Israelis kill the pirates, which they will, they can expect the full support of their government, unlike the British.

After the Malacca Straits, we were on the open run to Sri Lanka. The weather was nice and, as we'd already cleaned the tanks, we were able to wind down a bit. The Thai chipping team were on board now and they were using all the air hammers, and so we weren't doing a lot of that.

They were an easy-going lot. They were allowed one tiny messroom and one hot ring and an occasional bag of rice and a few vegetables. Occasionally, they might be seen watching videos in the crew messroom, but the sailors were about equally divided into two sets holding opposing views: those inclined to be kind to them, and the out and out racists. The Thais soon got sick of being invited in by one, and then, thirty minutes later, being slung out by another. Of course, they were never allowed anywhere near the officers' messroom, but then neither were the British A.B.s.

We washed the decks with the fire monitors which were stationed along the catenary. That was fun. The temptation to point the monitor at someone was huge. Out of the corner of my eye, I saw the mate peering from his window. By now, he'd decided that he didn't like us cadets very much, and I suddenly knew that he was waiting for one of us to do this so that he could fire the culprit. It would have been a pretty stupid thing for someone to do because it might have washed someone off the deck and over the side, but it would have been an easy mistake to make if you weren't thinking straight. It would have been more professional of him just to warn us not to do it.

The crossing to Sri Lanka was balmy but as usual, just when things were low key and calm, politics reared its ugly head. Through my new friend, the steward, I found out all about it. The mate, who had been working like a maniac towards this goal for years, was due to be promoted to captain when the captain went home. So far, so good, for him. Then the company proposed to send out its most useless officer to replace him. The captain didn't want to see him come on board and was insisting that he was incompetent. The mate wanted to take the chance on having him so that he could get to be captain ASAP even though he was a little bit worried. The captain wouldn't let him. They'd thought that the company would simply send someone else out in Jeddah, but the company, probably annoyed, was being difficult and saying that it couldn't find someone else until we got to New Jersey, our destination after Jeddah. What now? The captain and the mate could hardly go back to the company and say that they'd had a radical rethink and decided that the relief mate first proposed was actually a brilliant guy after all. The captain would have to stay longer, and the mate would have to wait for his promotion.

Added to that, the second mate was due

off and the captain had vetoed the promotion of the third mate on the grounds that he thought he was incompetent, too. That meant that the company had to find another second mate.

The steward knew all this because all communication was by letter from home and telex from the company. He cleaned the officers' cabins and the officers left their letters lying around and the captain left the telexes lying around and the steward read all of them. Stupidly, he put himself at risk by letting the third mate know what was happening. If the third mate had decided to protest to the captain, there would have been a big scene over how he had found out.

The third mate confided in me, but I didn't know what to say. He annoyed me at other times in any case. He really didn't know anything about the cargo system and he would ask a question out on deck on how to do something during cargo operations and if I didn't have the information, he would snap. He'd had a right old go at me in Yokohama over an incident to do with the mail, too. The idiot girl in the office had sent the post out without telling the Japanese agent that the ship had changed its name. The Japanese agent had just thought they'd been a mistake and sent all the post back. She was a complete plank. I'd laughed when the third mate said that if the company couldn't organise this, what hope was there, because I'd thought he was making a joke, and he hadn't liked it. This girl was pretty stupid. She'd once rung up a mate who was supposed to be joining a ship in Sydney and told him that she'd asked the travel agency to book him a ticket to Melbourne and that he could get a bus up. When he asked her why she hadn't had him booked on a flight to Sydney, she had said, "Well, I looked at the map and Sydney didn't look big enough to have an airport, so I said Melbourne." I don't think she'd ever been off the Isle of Man in her life. You had to be careful what you said, though. All the winding-down captains working in the office were very defensive of her.

The mate and the third mate continued in their moodiness. The captain wandered around, his hair greying by the hour. The second mate continued drinking and sobering up, over and over again, oblivious to all this.

When we finally did round Sri Lanka, I saw a speedboat with a lot of gunmen in it, circling us. I ran up to the bridge to tell the second mate.

He just shrugged. "But aren't we supposed to take precautions?" I asked.

"Such as?" he said, languidly.

"You know," I replied, "fire hoses, that sort of thing."

"My wife's not on board," he said, "and they're welcome to all the company's money in the safe and they're not going to steal this old rust bucket, so they won't slit our throats and throw us overboard."

Exasperated, I went out on deck again. The guys in the speedboat gave me a disdainful look and sped off back to shore. Well, that was a damp squib, I thought.

I wouldn't have had much of a story for the newspapers anyway. The Government was still suppressing news of pirate attacks at that time.

They suppressed a lot of things

concerning the Merchant Navy. They'd asked a second mate to take notes on the Yellow river years ago and after he'd been arrested of spying (of which, he was obviously guilty) and flung in jail by the Chinese and, subsequent to his eventual release months later, upon his arrival at Heathrow, he'd replied to a newsman, who had asked him why he'd done it, that the British Government had asked him to. He was immediately bundled into a toilet by his handlers and emerged a minute later, stating that the Government hadn't asked him to.

We crossed the Arabian Sea, still enjoying good weather and then entered the Red Sea. The captain hated Arabs and took every opportunity to let everyone know this. He also hated black people. He'd spent all his adult life and a large part of his juvenile life stuck on ships and I didn't understand how he'd got too know any of these ethnic minorities well enough to be able to decide that he hated them.

Jeddah was another disappointment. It was just an oil terminal. We weren't allowed off. I thought we might see something romantic similar to a scene from Lawrence of Arabia perhaps. We only saw two Arab people, the agent and the security guard. The agent at least did his best to look the part, arriving in a flowing white robe.

The captain was worried that alcohol might be found other than in the bond. The alcoholics would have it hidden all over the ship. The second mate cheerfully announced that he'd had a copy of The Satanic Verses but had left it lying around and couldn't remember where. I thought he might be joking. It was difficult to tell with him. The captain's brow furrowed, but he didn't push him. The second mate might be serious but thinking of a different ship.

The shore representative for the refinery was a young, ginger-haired Englishman, an ex-mate from tankers. He was full of how much money he was making. "Twenty thousand, tax free," he kept saying. The mate, who was very tight and always on about money, was on the same wavelength, and they got on. I was thinking, twenty thousand a year, to be stuck out here, is it really worth it.

For comparison, the mate was on about the same, the third mate was on thirteen, the captain was on about twenty-five.

It was difficult to get rich working in the Merchant Navy. In the old days, until about nineteen seventy-five, captains had done all right. The pay was high relative to that in other occupations, and they could expect to retire to a nice villa overlooking a river or the sea in Devon or somewhere similar.

The problem was competition. Why would a company pay a moaning Englishman twice the pay to do the same job as they would have to pay a Bombay Indian. It was claimed by the British officers that they worked longer hours, felt more obligation to the company, and were better in emergencies, but the companies didn't care about that.

The British merchant seamen were an early casualty of globalisation. The Government didn't care about them. The third officer had more or less been thrown out of his local M.P.'s constituency surgery when he went to complain. But, of course, with time, other industries would follow including ones the

Government did care about, but the politicians were either too short-sighted, too selfish, or too unintelligent to see this.

We were soon full and on our way again. The authorities hadn't found any alcohol stashes or the missing copy of The Satanic Verses. We'd had no crew changes. The second mate was now overdue to go home and would soon be hitting the bottle even harder. The captain was overdue too but that was his own fault for being self-righteous over the proposed relief mate.

The Suez Canal, the Mediterranean and Gibraltar

We went up to Suez. When the pilot turned up, the third mate had been waiting for him. There was a lot of shouting. The captain sent me down from the bridge to assist. I found the pilot standing on deck at the top of the pilot ladder, looking offended. There was no one else around. He started to have a go at me. He sounded quite pompous, actually. I took him up to the bridge and introduced him to the captain, and then the bridge door opened, and a flustered third mate came in. "He wanted a heaving line for his briefcase," he whispered to me. "I offered him the orange line from the lifebuoy, but he wasn't satisfied with that and I went off to find a heaving line and then I came back and he'd gone."

We more or less owned all these countries, I thought, and now they're bossing us around. Where would they have been without the British Empire. All right, Egypt wasn't technically part of the Empire, but it in effect was.

The ship moved into the Suez Canal. I was put on the wheel. I had to admire the pilot's skill. The canal is not very wide yet he was slinging the ship around the bends. So far as I knew, he'd never been on this ship before and even if he had, there was no way he could have remembered its characteristics and yet he knew exactly when to give helm orders so that the ship finished up dead in the middle, exactly on course.

The captain stayed up on the bridge the whole time. On the regular runs around Europe on which I later worked, the captains would slope off. Even on the runs where the captains had pilotage exemptions, they would give their number over the radio to the river control and then slope off, or just tell you to give their number and not come up at all.

The captain was obligated to stay though when you think about it. He hadn't had anything else to do apart from sit in his cabin for months. This was in the time before emails had come in and every idiot in the office could bombard the captain with emails whenever he felt like it.

The thing I was to find about native pilots was that you couldn't really have a conversation. If you had a Western pilot, you had the chance of a conversation with someone new which was a real shot in the arm after months with the same people who, try as they might, couldn't help talking about the same things.

The boat filled up with more bum boat people. There were only men this time, no prostitutes. Some were kind of technically employed, such as the people to operate the Suez light, which we had to rig even though it was daylight. Their products weren't of a very high quality. The sailors always considered a Singaporean fake Lacoste polo shirt to be a cut above an Egyptian fake Lacoste polo shirt.

There was some negotiation with the

mate and the chief engineer over scrap. The second engineer wouldn't have anything to do with this. I suppose with the new garbage regulations, this has all changed. How are you going to explain what you did with all those old parts if you can't produce a signed receipt from a shore reception facility.

I peered out of the external door from our alleyway and saw the mate and chief engineer in earnest conversation with some of the Egyptians.

Eventually, once we were through, I was sent up to the bow and found the ship towing one of the bum boats. The Egyptians had hold of one end of the rope, and the other was still tied to the bitts on deck. This bum boat was practically surfing as we pulled it along. The bosun was there. "What's going on?" I asked him. He ignored me and went to the rail.

"It's not me," he said to the Egyptians. He pointed at the mate. "It's him," he continued. He turned a worried face to me. "They'll put the ju-ju on me," he said.

It turned out that they were to be given the rope but had sworn at the mate, and he wouldn't let them have it now. "They're not getting it after what they said to me," said the mate in his, hard-nosed, Northern manner. Finally, the bum boat men gave up and threw their end of the line into the water. The mate had a satisfied smile on his face.

I went back to the bridge to see the captain presenting the pilot with his thousands of Marlboro, without a supply of which you cannot transit the Suez Canal. I didn't think the Marlboro were the pilot's official pay. It's strange how these countries let this go on. They just hold back their own development. It would be so much simpler for commerce to flourish if they just cleaned it all up. But then the Western countries stifle their own commerce with over-regulation.

We cruised through the Mediterranean. There wasn't a lot to see. Some of the older sailors lamented the fate of the Med. "It was teeming with life in the fifties and sixties," they said. We didn't see any sea life.

The weather stayed good, but we weren't given any time off for working on our pay-off tans. You couldn't work without a shirt on out on deck; you'd get covered in dirt and clippings and oil. We fumed about the mate. Little did we know that his replacement would be far worse.

At Gibraltar, we took on bunkers at anchor. There was no shore leave. The captain either couldn't be bothered to organise launches or the company wouldn't pay for them or the Gibraltarians didn't want sailors ashore. It would be impolitic to ask which. "That rock is full of chemical weapons and God knows what else," said the second mate.

"Really?" I said.

"Of course," he answered. "That's why we can't give it back. Anyway, it was Arabic originally. We should give it to Morocco if we give it to anyone. And what about Melilla and Ceuta?" What were Melilla and Ceuta. I had no idea. It turned out they were Spanish enclaves in North Africa.

The engineers fumed while they took bunkers. They hated working out on deck and they hated working when the deck officers had nothing to do. I was often stunned by their bitterness.

The Atlantic and the Storm

Finally, we were full of bunkers and were to set out across the Atlantic. The captain was looking worried. The weather reports weren't good. "We're on a two-hundred metre tanker," I said to the second mate.

"You'd be surprised what you can find yourself going through," he said.

"But all those little yachts?" I asked him.

"Yeah, they cross," he said. "But the owners who don't make it don't write the books."

For the first few days, everything was all right. The sailors, though, were looking a little bit worried, and until then I'd never seen them looking worried.

I began to wonder. Surely everyone was over-worried. We weren't on a windjammer.

The captain was spending more time on the bridge and the mate was working even more efficiently than normal, which he always did when he thought there was something in the air.

Then the storm hit us. It just got worse and worse. The ship rolled violently due to the heavy centre of gravity it had, being fully loaded, and it pitched heavily too. The bow was rising to the level of the bridge and then crashing down on top of the waves.

At the storm's height, I went up to the bridge. The captain was standing as stiff as a board, staring out at the spray and waves crashing over the deck. The third mate was on watch with him. He seemed to be enjoying it. It was the second mate's opinion you really wanted. He was the most stable one, if you left his alcoholism out of it. The previous afternoon, he'd shrugged off the storm. "If the bow were going to fall off, it would have done it in the Pacific," he'd said.

It was quite clear how pointless all that lifesaving training at Warsash had been. The chances of getting into a liferaft or a lifeboat and surviving in this were, I was confident, nil.

The real danger in storms is that the deck coamings come off and then the holds or tanks start filling, but we were full anyway. It'd have to be something immediately catastrophic to sink us, such as splitting in half. It was the bulk carriers that were most at risk. They sometimes had lots of space in their holds even when down to their marks and they weren't as strong, having been subjected to far higher stresses throughout their working lives. At this time, one was going down every fortnight, all barely reported by the newspapers of course, their readers not generally being interested in the fate of a gang of Filipinos on the other side of the world.

The mate sent me to see how the other cadet was. He was lying in his shower with his mouth over the drain, vomiting. "Can I help?" I asked him. He swore at me.

I bumped into the mate in an alleyway. I told him that I'd found the other cadet vomiting in his shower and he had sworn at me so I left him to it. The mate was indignant.

"We do have stuff we can give him you

know," he said.

"He swore at me and told me to get out," I said. "What do you want me to do? Tell me and I'll do it."

He huffed and walked off. He didn't bother going to see the other cadet himself, though.

We spent a whole day just hove to. Finally, the storm started to die down and we put a little bit of speed on her.

The mate was sent up to the fo'c'sle to look for damage, and I accompanied him. He whistled when we walked in. All the pillars which held the mooring deck up were bent like bananas.

"The waves crushed the mooring deck," I said.

"It's worse," said the mate. "The bottom of the hull's been bent up."

"All that smacking down on the surface?" I asked. The mate didn't bother answering me. Obviously, it was the smacking down on the surface.

He had a poke around. "Come on," he said. "There's nothing more to see here, and nothing we can do. Let's go and deliver the bad news to the old man. You keep your mouth shut. I know you. You'll burst in and start gabbing away." I followed him up the deck in silence.

The captain looked very worried. The second mate was up and around. "The company's likely to blame him," he said to me, quietly, after the news had been delivered.

"It's not his fault," I answered.

"He's the captain; everything is his fault," said the second mate. "If he'd gone around the weather or slowed down, the company would have blamed him for costing them money. Now that he's gone through it and there's damage, the company will blame him for the damage. The company is a rotten organisation. All shipping companies are, at least since the days of the old British family companies. He's a newish captain, too," he continued.

"Maybe they'll put it down to inexperience," I suggested.

"Shut up," he hissed. "You think you can pass judgement on the captain?"

"I only said...," I began. He hissed again.

"You just don't know when to keep quiet do you?" he said.

Actually, the plight of captains faced with bad weather has become quite ridiculous. There was one notorious court case which went on for years. The charterers always try to force captains to traverse the high latitudes when you cross the North Pacific from North America, with the idea that you will get pushed along by the tops of the highs. One captain took his ship by the southern route, despite the charterers insisting on the northern route. The charterers sued because that cost them more money. The courts backed them. So, everyone thought, the captain is not responsible for the consequences of this. Ah, said the court, he is still responsible; he just doesn't have the authority to ignore the terms of the charter. This is what it is like being a captain these days, being judged by inexperienced, spotty adolescent accountants, the judiciary in nice safe old London and pen-pushing, ponces on society, with clipboards and official stamps.

New Jersey

We arrived at the pilot station for New Jersey. The pilot was the usual, miserable, arrogant, American pilot. He caused some confusion within moments of coming on board. "Captain," he said, "be sure to tell your guys not to shout at the mooring men." The message was duly relayed to us at our mooring stations. Why would we shout at them, we wondered, and why can't we shout at them.

When the tugs finally pushed us alongside, we saw why. The mooring men were all over seventy. They worked their arthritic way along the quay, at their own pace. You almost expected them to pause for a whiff of oxygen from a tank. "What's going on?" I asked the second mate, who was down there with us. "What are they doing employing this lot?"

"This is the northern United States," he said. "It's all unionised. The authority won't be able to fire them even if they're ninety and in bath chairs."

"I thought it might be because they're all connected to the Mafia?" I said. He shrugged.

"That might be true, too," he said. "Again, this is the States."

It took forever for them to tie us up. I could see some of the sailors were dying to shout at them. I wanted to know what would happen if they did. The mooring men would probably just throw the lines aside and stomp off, sulking.

We didn't see anything of New Jersey. The shoreline looked like a dump, but commercial shorelines normally do.

The new mate and second mate were standing on the quay with the agent. They were both rotund and looked like jolly guys. How deceptive appearances can be.

A Ford Mustang rolled up with some guys in it, and, as soon as it was rigged, the young sailor went down the accommodation ladder to join them and go for a spin. They were some friends of his from his backpacking days.

Both I and the other cadet worked on getting the manifold set up for the cargo and then we went into the cargo room. The new mate was there with the current mate. The new mate smiled. Eagerly, we asked if there was a chance of getting a watch off so that we could get into New York City. The old mate passed the question on to the new mate "No," said the new mate. The old mate looked surprised but just shrugged.

We went out on deck again. We couldn't believe it. We were so close to Manhattan and we weren't going to see it. Getting there and back, in and out of the refinery, on the six hours between watches, wasn't practical.

This policy of working cadets flat out is a bit self-defeating on the part of the companies. They soon tire of seeing no more than one oil refinery after another, but you can see the mate's point. Nothing to be gained by him in letting us go. Better for him to keep us on board: extra pairs of hands.

Some people said, "Well, if you weren't here, he'd have to manage without you, so why can't he now." His point would be, why should he.

Nothing for it but to keep on alternating working and sleeping and hope we didn't run down too much before we left.

The Americans didn't want to speak to us Brits. They were probably still fuming over our attempt to charge them taxes for protecting them from the French and for attempting to prevent them from massacring the Indians and stealing their land. The Texans were much friendlier. Texas was like a different country. I didn't understand why the Texans didn't just become independent.

The new second mate and I were put on watch together. He was in his mid-thirties, unfit, had been working ashore for ten years and lived in Venezuela. Venezuela was well known at the time for winning Miss World every other year.

Once he started going on about his wife, which he soon did, I quietly asked to see a photo. She was not much to look at. I wondered why these men went to live in these tropical places and then didn't marry a stunner when you considered that they could have anyone they wanted. I think it was because they convinced themselves that if their women weren't beautiful then they must really love them. In truth, their women probably didn't love them any more than a stunner would; it was just easier for their men to convince themselves that they did.

He never moved out of the cargo room. Luckily, by now, I knew enough to virtually do all the cargo watch by myself. I brought him the figures every hour and he would copy them into the cargo log. Once he'd stopped going on about his wife, his only comment to me was that I wrote the tanks down in the wrong order. "But I've written the tanks numbers next to the ullages," I said.

"Yes, but you should write the figures on the paper in the pattern of the tanks on deck," he said. I missed the other second mate already.

There was a clattering and I knew it was the captain's bulk coming down the internal stairway. He looked into the crew mess. He was wearing a fake Lacoste polo shirt, a Singaporean one: only the best for him.

He was going home. He looked at me as if wondering whether I merited a goodbye. He considered that I did. The second mate had stood up and grasped a red pen in his hand, clearly hoping that he looked officious and efficient. The captain wished him good luck and he was gone.

So now the old mate was the new captain.

The new mate quickly decided he didn't like him and began to refer to him as 'Captain Marvel' behind his back. We didn't like this. He'd been a good mate even if he were prone to the odd, irrational outburst and was a bit officious, and he would have given us a watch off, that was certain.

I wondered if the sailors would take a dislike to the new mate and kill him. Then I realized that I might be going out of my mind.

It was odd to see the old mate sitting in the captain's cabin. He looked very confident. He was quite tough. The only thing was he'd made a few enemies, the third mate being one of them, and now, being a new captain, the last thing he needed around him was juniors with a score to settle.

The new second mate was obsequious to him. "Captain, I hope you don't mind but I'd just like to know whether you want me to call you by your first name or captain?" I heard him asking in a grovelling voice. Just call him captain, I thought. Why are you even asking.

The engineers all managed to get ashore and the third mate did, too, as the old second mate was still on board so covered one of his watches.

They all came back late at night, as did the young sailor, and regaled us with stories of Manhattan. The old second mate saw that I was looking a bit gloomy. "Listen," he said, "you're just doing your cadetship on a scrap tanker, same as we all had to. When you get your ticket, get yourself on a nice cruise ship."

Out on deck, things did not go all that well. We were used to having a super-efficient mate, and this new guy wasn't that good. Adding to the problems was that, even though it may have been justified, the old mate and new captain, just couldn't leave the cargo operation alone and kept interfering.

"Everyone's tired," said the third mate. "It's been nearly five months now. Everyone's worn out."

Five months doesn't sound a long time, but when you're cooped up in what is only a maximum-security prison with a very airy exercise yard, and living with vibration and machinery noise day in, day out, it can become a bit of a strain.

Finally, we'd got rid of our Saudi Arabian cargo and got another pilot on board and went out into the river. A little workboat came out with some acetylene bottles for the engineers, and we lifted them onboard. The bosun and the sailors rolled the bottles out of their cage and then told the tug driver to go away.

"I want the lifting cage back," he shouted up.

"We're too busy, we'll send it back from Texas," shouted the bosun, our destination having been recently decided.

"I want it now," shouted the American. "Get those Filipinos to send it down if you're too busy. He pointed to the Thais who were hanging over the bulwark watching.

"They're not Filipinos; they're Thais," I shouted down, pretending I was trying to be helpful. The bosun stared at me. "I'm just trying to clarify things," I said. The American was screaming obscenities by now.

Eventually, the mate appeared and told the bosun to just send the cage down. The pilot had probably intervened.

The cage was delivered, and we slid out of New Jersey.

To the Gulf and Houston

The run down to the Gulf was fairly peaceful. The captain (ex-mate) was looking even stiffer than normal. This was what he'd worked for since he'd left school.

All his little pens were lined up; his notepads were nice and tidy.

I walked past his cabin once and the young sailor was in there moaning that he was being kept on after Texas. "But I did over my time last trip," he was complaining. The captain tried to mollify him. When I would become a captain, I would find the same thing: you just sit there with your new stripes, wondering what the world will bring, and, the next moment, you find out. Moaning crew is what it brings.

The third mate was being kept on after Texas, too. This was adding insult to injury. They'd passed him over for promotion and now they were keeping him on over his time. It was a further insult that the new second mate had been working ashore for a long time and hadn't been on a tanker for fourteen years but was considered by the company to be a better candidate for the job than he.

I tried to console him. He always insisted that he was the only true seamen on the boat and he might have been right. Being from the West Country, he had always been around boats. As soon as you did anything to do with ropes and the like, you saw that straight away.

The old mate (new captain) despite being highly intelligent, always looked lost during mooring operations and the old captain had been from some town in Mid-Yorkshire and seemed more interested in going on and on about Arthur Scargill than anything else, half the time.

There was a new third engineer on board. He was a little guy in his mid-thirties and what is called a professional third. They spend their whole working lives at sea in that rank and have no ambition to go any higher. They can be highly competent, they just don't want to get bogged down in writing reports and worrying about bunkers and don't want to go back to college and study all those difficult subjects such as heat.

I got on well with him. He was a bit of a bad influence though, and the other engineers didn't like him, and I wasn't doing myself any good by being friendly to him. The politics of life on board were so complicated.

We saw Miami beach. It was so sad, sailing past somewhere like that. If only we could drop anchor and all go ashore.

The Americans were never off the radio. They just loved calling each other up. If they didn't have anyone in particular to call, they would just start jabbering away, asking for a radio check. It was driving the third mate mad.

There was one female captain who kept calling people up, saying this is captain so and so, this is captain so and so, over and over again. I watched the third mate's face. Finally, he burst out with "We all know you're a captain, you don't have to keep telling the whole world." He started moving over to the VHF to tell her this. "I don't think that's a good idea," I said, and he left it alone.

Every non-American at sea had a morbid fear of the U.S. Coast Guard. They were notorious and generally thought of as being bureaucratic fascists who wouldn't listen and didn't know what they were doing. Once they had you in your sights, it was like being a person of interest to the Spanish Inquisition. It was best to avoid having any dealings with them, and you shouldn't do anything which might attract their attention.

Soon, we'd rounded Florida and were running up to Texas through the oil fields.

Oil rigs are a bit of a nuisance as the oil companies are forever moving them around. They're hazards to navigation if you think about it. So are their pipelines. And all the responsibility is on the seafarer, yet again. If you've been anchoring in a certain spot for years and the authorities let some oil company lay a pipeline there and you puncture it, it's your fault, and the authorities don't take into consideration the needs of shipping. It's always the case that the big oil companies get what the big oil companies want.

"I wonder how the captain's going to cope," said the third mate as we neared the pilot station. "I've seen a few chinks in his armour." The third mate was just dying to see him fail. This was his first port arrival as captain and the mate didn't seem all that proactive, so he didn't have fantastic back up.

Just then, the captain appeared on the bridge. He always seemed to do that when you were talking about him. "I'll see you in my cabin," he said to me.

I followed him down the internal

staircase wondering what he'd heard. I hadn't actually said anything about him, I'd only been listening. I was mentally preparing my defence.

We got in there, and he sat down and said, "I'm keeping you on for cargo operations."

"Oh, O.K," I said, relieved. He seemed to have been expecting some kind of protest.

"The company wanted to send you two (i.e. I and the other cadet) home upon arrival, but I'm keeping you on," he said. I shrugged.

"Who cares, anyway," I said. "We've been here for five months. What's another few days."

"It doesn't matter what you think?" he said. "No one cares what you think. You'll be staying until the end of cargo, and that's all there is to it."

What's wrong with him? I wondered. Was he losing it? Was the pressure of command getting to him already?

"Yes captain," I said.

"Run along," he told me.

I found the other cadet. "We're staying until the end of cargo and then going home," I said. He fumed.

"It's not fair," he insisted. I was mystified. Why this reaction. "I want to go home," he said.

"You are going home," I told him, "Just a few days later than you were hoping, that's all."

I went back up to the bridge and told the third mate all this. I thought he'd be relieved that the captain hadn't overheard what he'd been saying about him, but he didn't care what the captain had overheard him saying.

"So, the junior cadet has got the hump, has he?" he mused.

"He's not officially the junior cadet," I said.

"No, he's just a bit younger," he replied. "He doesn't like it if you try to tell him to do something and insists that you two are equal, but he won't want to go home on his own, will he."

"He isn't going home on his own," I said. The third mate smiled and picked up the phone and asked the other cadet to come to the bridge.

"Well," he said, when he'd arrived. "You want to go home upon arrival, so I'll see the captain and you can fly home early and Willy'll stay on his own to help with the cargo." The other cadet turned red and gave me a look of pure hate. "What's the matter?" said the third mate. "You don't want to travel on your own? You're independent, aren't you? You're your own man, or so you've been insisting for five months."

I was a bit lost. I hadn't realised that the third mate didn't like the other cadet. I knew everyone else didn't.

The other cadet slunk off the bridge. "We'll let him stew for a bit," said the third mate.

We pulled in to the same berth at which we'd joined five months previously. "Not bad," said one of the sailors to me as he walked past, "Your first trip and you've done a circumnavigation." I hadn't thought about this until then. Yes, he was right, and both canals too.

The dockers started complaining while we were rigging the gangway. They used their jeeps to pull the ropes along the quay and the oiler, who came up on deck once in a while to help us moor, had put the winch into reverse by mistake and instead of paying out the rope, allowing them to drag it along, had started heaving it in, and nearly pulled their jeep into the dock.

"Yeah, yeah," sorry about that," said the bosun.

"That guy ain't the brightest," they said, or something like that. The oiler had gone back to the engine room by now and it was safe to concur with them.

By now, we knew exactly what we were doing. We had all the tank valves set up, the correct pipes on the manifold, the p.v. valves all organised.

This mate was not one to give out praise, something the previous mate had done on occasion, but we were starting to take pride in our work. I did realise, though, that we'd learnt very little about actual seamanship. Really, we'd had five months training in how to be petrol station attendants.

There was the possibility of getting ashore here. The new mate wasn't going to give us any time off, that was sure, but if we worked our six hours, went ashore for six hours and then worked our next shift, we'd be all right.

The third mate and one of the sailors and I organised to go. Just as we were getting into the taxi, the other cadet turned up. "What are you doing?" I asked him. "Aren't you on watch?"

"The mate gave me the watch off," he said, cheerfully. Damn. The mate had probably done it just to make sure he ruined the third mate's and my little trip. There was no limit to spite in the Merchant Navy.

The third mate sighed, and we all climbed in.

After we'd done the rounds at the shopping centre, we went to some neighbourhood bar. The owner and his wife were friendly and assured us they were going to look after us and make sure we didn't get rolled.

The third mate got into conversation with a couple of girls, and the bar owner warned them off. "They'll just take you for drinks all night and then go home without you," he said. The third mate looked as if he were going to say he wouldn't mind just paying for their company, but the owner gave him a friendly slap on the shoulder and went back round the bar.

The other cadet drank heavily but, unfortunately, couldn't handle it. He was soon mouthing off about "Yanks," and imitating their accents at the top of his voice.

"Careful," I said.

"Why?" He demanded, indignantly.

"You'll get filled in," I said.

"Who by?" he wanted to know. "You?"

"Them," I said flicking my eyes around the bar. "Look around you. The shortest one is six foot.

He looked around him.

"I'm not scared," he said.

I turned to find the third mate to appeal to him, but he'd wormed his way back into the company of the girls whom the owner had warned off. I waited until the other cadet had turned round, and slid over to a table and sat on my own for a while.

Then a rather heavy lady sat down opposite me. "Hi, honey," she said. "Where y'all from?"

"I am all from England," I said. She looked blank. "It's a small island off the coast of Europe," I added.

"You want to come back to my motel?" she said. I thought about it.

"How far away is it?" I asked.

"Not far," she said.

"Sure, why not?" I told her.

I saw the third mate look up at me as I went out the door. I waved to him, and he smiled.

"What are you doing here?" I asked the woman as we trudged through the grass verge, there being no pavement.

"I'm a truck driver, honey," she said.

"There are lady truck drivers in the States?" I asked, astonished.

"Yeah, aren't there in England?" she said.

"I don't think so," I told her.

She swung open the door to her motel apartment and I could see a bath through the bathroom door. I'd spent five months having to wash myself in a shower that, due to a faulty mixer tap, was either freezing cold or scalding hot, and I just walked straight in and started running the bath.

Unthinkingly, I shut the bathroom door. I was in such bliss that I forgot I was with someone.

Half an hour later, I reappeared in the living room. "I think you'd better leave," the woman drawled.

I looked at her. She seemed quite determined. It was best not to argue. American police shot first and asked questions afterwards, didn't they. Best just to slip out quietly.

I stood in the forecourt and wondered where I was. I couldn't even remember the name of the bar. Luckily, I'd taken the precaution of writing down the address of the oil terminal and I went into the motel office and asked them to ring me a taxi.

"You're going to love this ride," said the receptionist.

"Oh yeah, why?" I asked.

"This is the Cadillac taxi company I'm dialling," she said. Oh great, I thought. This is going to cost a fortune.

Half an hour later, a complete wreck of a car rolled up, very slowly. "That's a Cadillac?" I said.

"Sure is, boy," said the driver, getting out.

I turned up at the terminal and climbed the accommodation ladder to the ship's deck. The new second mate was in the cargo office. He'd left his watchman to look after the cargo. He must have been mad. Any mistake and he'd have been blamed and hauled off by the authorities. This wasn't a proper cargo control room with tank gauges from which it was O.K. to do a watch. It was just a desk in front of the pump switchboard.

I changed into my orange boiler suit and went outside even though I wasn't officially on watch for a few hours. There didn't seem to be any point in just lying in my bunk.

This was still the other cadet's watch officially.

He and the third mate rolled up at ten to midnight. The sailor who'd gone ashore with us wasn't with them.

The other cadet was very unsteady and

the third mate had to guide him through the obstacles on deck.

"How'd you get on with those girls?" I asked the third mate.

"Great," he said. "Bought them loads of drinks and then we had to leave."

"See them again?" I said.

"Nah," he replied. "I won't get off again."

The sailor on watch came up to me. "You know where we're going?" he said.

"No," I replied. "The second mate hadn't mentioned anything.

"Rio," he said, with a satisfied smile.

"Damn," I said. I wanted to go to Rio.

Still, I thought, it would have been the same old story: no time off, trying to see something in six hours between watches, which included travelling time to and from the refinery. But then, if you followed that logic, what was the point in travelling at all

This loading a cargo without knowing in advance where you were taking it wasn't unusual. Cargos could be bought and sold a hundred times before you reached your destination in some cases, if say you were heading for the Gibraltar Straits, or in the general direction of North America.

There had been a nasty surprise for the engineers. The company had suddenly organised a classification-society survey. They'd been hoping to get away to Gillie's. Of course, they were fuming, some of the deck department having got off the boat when they wouldn't have the chance. They never liked that.

I walked into the crew bar and the second engineer swore at me and told me to get out. It was best to avoid them when they were in a bad mood, anyway. The new third engineer wasn't too vicious, just morose. He hadn't been on that long.

This is just another of those things now. Companies are always wrecking your schemes for going ashore. They even have you slow down on your trips so that you don't cost them unnecessary expensive alongside time. If you were to examine the U.N. Treaties on treatment of refugees, I am sure that they wouldn't tolerate keeping them cooped up for months and months without the occasional trip outside their compound. Yet the U.N. is quite happy for merchant seamen to receive this treatment.

The captain was bouncing around full of energy. He'd had his first port as Capitano in New Jersey and there'd been no disaster and his first port arrival in Houston and there'd been no disaster there either.

I thought more about the ship going to Rio after Texas. I still didn't know whether to be glad I was going home for a few weeks or disappointed about missing out on Rio.

I sat in the cargo office with the second mate, listening to him talking about Venezuela and his wife. "She's not a prostitute," he said, defensively.

"I never said she was," I told him.

"So, don't go thinking she is," he said. I sighed. Some of these people were quite mad.

I tried changing the subject. "So, were you always in the Merchant Navy?" I asked him.

"I started out in a surveyor's office," he said. "Then I told my father I didn't like it and I went onto P and O. They sent me on a long trip and then, when we got back to King George Vth dock, they said I had to do some coasting, and I didn't want to stay, and when the registrar came to sign me onto the coastal agreement, I said, 'Haven't you heard, I'm going home,' and he said, 'Oh,' and signed me off, and I went home, and my family took me out to the theatre, and then I thought again and I rang up and said can I come back and they said , 'Yes,' but I said, 'Please can I not have to do the coasting,' but they made me do it. That was in the sixties."

It was the first time he'd ever spoken at length, other than about Venezuela and his wife. I tried to draw him out more, but he slumped back into his customary mode of indifference to company. If I had been to Venezuela then, I would have pumped him for more information on how to immigrate. I went years later for half a day, working on a cruise ship, and managed to get a few hours in Caracas. I was so overwhelmed by the sight of incredible looking women in white spandex, stomping through Bolivar Square, that I decided to take refuge in MacDonald's, only to find that every girl working behind the tills looked like she could be a Miss World, too. I thought about emigrating there then, that's for certain.

The mate wandered around in his silent way. I still didn't know if I liked him. He was still being a bit snide about the captain and he hadn't done me any favours, but, on the other hand, he didn't go out of his way to make you suffer.

He had to go to the captain for advice at one stage, and the captain, with his customary efficiency, knew exactly what was wrong and sorted everything out immediately. That was embarrassing for him after he'd been slagging the captain off.

The engineers could be seen running around with the surveyor. They still fumed. The surveyor seemed a bit taken aback by their hostility which couldn't even be put down to anti-Americanism as he was British. I saw him trying a new strategy to make things less uncomfortable and friendlier. He started slagging off the Americans, but the engineers were so disgruntled that even this reliable old standby didn't work.

"There's another company in our building and they decided that every visitor to our building had to sign a visitor's book. We wouldn't do it, so they tried to stop us coming into our own offices, so we said, 'Right, we'll get our own book and you'll have to sign our book'," he said. He looked at the engineers' faces, hoping for a flicker of a smile. There was none. I started to feel a bit sorry for him. It wasn't his fault that the company didn't organize things so that they had time to go up the road.

The cargo operations were going smoothly. The young sailor was bouncing around, over excited about going to Rio. "I'm paying off in Rio, too, I'll get a few days in a hotel," he said. An, older, more cynical sailor, standing by the manifold with us, said, quietly, "No you won't, the company won't spend a cent on a hotel for you if there's the slightest chance of dumping you straight on a flight and, even if they do, they'll put you in some dump you'll be lucky to get out of alive." The young sailor wasn't listening.

When I handed over to the other cadet he said, "The captain wants to see you."

I went up to his cabin. He was sitting

there with his different coloured biros lined up neatly in front of him, sorting through some papers. He slung my discharge book across to me. "I'm sending you home tomorrow," he said. I waited to see if he had anything else to say such as, good luck, or see you again. He just carried on shuffling his papers. I turned to leave. "Just a minute," he said. Aha. I turned back. "Make sure your cabin is clean."

I saw the other cadet in the crew mess, later on. "Did the captain wish you good luck?" I asked him. He looked worried.

"No," he said. "Why did he you? I knew he didn't like me."

"He didn't which me good luck, either," I said.

The third mate was there. He slagged the captain off. "You get away from him tomorrow," he said. "I've got till Rio with him."

At least you know you won't have a disaster with him," I said.

"Yeah, not a cargo disaster but he's not a seaman," said the third mate. I remembered when, as mate, the captain had had me heaving on a little line with the winch which was attached to a big mooring rope. I could see it was going to snap and told him. "Keep heaving," he'd insisted. A moment later, it did snap, and struck me in the face. "Stop malingering," he'd said.

It came to three hours before the agent was due to take us to the airport. American immigration had already stamped all our papers. My cargo watch was starting. I waited for someone to tell me not to bother. No one did.

I went out on deck and took over from the other cadet while the third mate handed over to the second mate.

The bosun's wife was beckoning him from outside the accommodation entrance. He looked up at her and then over at me. "More shopping, Willy," he said quietly. "Don't ever get married, boy. Wait till we get to Rio, that'll cost me some I can tell you."

"I thought she was flying home with us," I said.

"That was until she heard about Rio," he replied. Damn, did that mean there'd been an option to stay on longer if you wanted. She wasn't staff, but even so. Maybe if I'd asked. Still, it was too late now. He walked away to see what she wanted.

"Tight git," said the third mate.

"What do you mean?" I asked him.

"He's saving on heating bills, food bills etc... That's the only reason people bring their wives away." So cynical. Still, if anyone was entitled to comment, it was the third mate. He was the only one who didn't regard fake Lacoste polo shirts as formal wear and even more annoyingly, insist that anyone wearing anything different was scruffy. I thought the bosun did genuinely love his wife.

"Who are you flying with?" said the third mate, changing the subject.

"British Airways," I said.

"Snooty stewardesses," he commented. "Still, at least you can be more confident of reaching your destination than you can on some of these American airlines."

He and the other cadet went away, leaving me with the second mate. A few moments later and the second mate said, "Well, if you need me, I'll be in the cargo office," and sloped off. Bloody hell, I thought. He's paid to be out here, not in there, reading a paperback. If that was me and I knew the cadet was getting off in three hours, I won't leave him out here in some orange boiler suit, getting bitten by mosquitoes.

A while later, I took the hourly figures in to the second mate. The captain was standing in the cargo room. "What are you doing?" He demanded. "Your car's coming soon. You should be ready. Don't think anyone's waiting around for the likes of you." The second mate shifted, guiltily.

"I'll get changed immediately," I said.

"See that you do," said the captain. I waited until I was out of sight and sighed.

"Willy, you still here?" said one of the sailors in the alleyway.

"Going home eh, all right for some," said one of the engineers.

I tidied all my stuff up in my suitcase, hung my boiler suit up, gave the shower a final rinse and went back to the officers' messroom.

The other cadet was sitting there, his hair in a neat side parting, his wispy moustache combed out. He looked even more like a nineteen-thirties caricature than normal.

"I'll be glad to get home," he said.

"Oh," Was all I could think of to say.

"Will you be coming back?" he asked.

"Yeah sure, why not?" I asked him.

"I want a normal life," he said.

"Millions of people have normal lives," I told him, "and they never stop moaning about them."

"I want a family," he said.

"You should have thought about all that

first," I said. "What do you care about a normal life? Just sail around on ships and go and lie on beaches when you're not signed on." He slumped.

The young sailor appeared in the doorway, all excited.

"Your car's here," he said. The other cadet and I smiled and went out and down the accommodation ladder.

I took a look at the ship, it's rust-stained hull making it look abandoned. That was my home for five months.

I was still looking at it over my shoulder as we drove slowly along the quay and then we turned around a row of tanks and a confluence of pipelines, and it was out of sight.

.

Printed in Great Britain
by Amazon

74466299R00092